How To Be The

Perfect Housewife

Entertain in Style

Anthea Turner

How To Be The Perfect Housewife

Entertain in Style

Anthea Turner

Virgin BOOKS

To Kate Waters, who taught me how to dress a salmon

First published in Great Britain in 2008 by
Virgin Books Ltd
Thames Wharf Studios
Rainville Road
London
W6 9HA

A catalogue record for this book is available from the British Library.

ISBN 978 07535 1332 3

Designed by Virgin Books Ltd.

Printed and bound in the UK by Butler and Tanner

Contents

INTRODUCTION

Parties, parties, parties . . . How we love to attend them, but arranging them ourselves? Phew! For some, social gatherings, however small, are a nightmare of gigantic proportions. For others – 'The Party Professionals' – they're a joy.

The key to this golden chalice of home making is enthusiasm, organisation and preparation. In this book I hope to give you all the help and encouragement I can, without actually turning up on your doorstep and doing it for you.

It's people who make a home – those who live in it and those who visit. I'm sure, like me, you have been to houses that are shining examples of co-ordination, design and cleanliness but for some reason feel unwelcoming. There are many reasons for this, but the most common is unhappy, uptight, unsociable occupants. What makes a house a home has nothing to do with money; a real home is one whose doors are open to friends dropping in for anything from a simple cup of coffee to a full-blown dinner party.

Like many things in life, what you put into your home you get back ten fold. I love to hear my house ringing with the voices of friends, but I'm happy to admit that things don't always go to plan. Summer barbecues have been a wash out, the oven has packed in as I'm about to roast a beautifully prepared fillet, ornaments have been broken, and children and animals have done what only they do best, but over the years I've learnt to cope with all sorts of social situations and to this day I still relish learning from others.

I'm not a cook, but I'm extremely competent with a few good books (I've listed some of my favourites at the end of this one). I'm not an interior designer, but I am an accomplished home maker. And I'm not a professional party planner but, since 1978 when, with two other friends, I arranged the St Dominic's Grammar School for Girls end-of-term dance (it was a blast), I have always put my best foot forward when it comes to entertaining.

Not everything in this book will be for you, but I hope that, when faced with a party, my trusty commonsense entertaining tips will be your saving grace.

With love

Anthea Turner x

CHAPTER 1
PARTY PREPARATION

Every successful hostess has two secret weapons in her armoury: preparation and the Perfect Housewife's greatest ally – loads of lists. That's how she glides, calmly and elegantly, through her entertaining. And so can you.

Entertain in Style is the only book the Perfect Housewife needs to throw the perfect party and have fun without feeling frazzled. It will show you how to make your parties the ones no one can bear to miss – modern, chic, sparkling, simple but memorable – without breaking the bank.

You'll find all the help you need to organise all kinds of fabulous occasions from the simple to the formal, as well as quick and easy recipes and menus. There's general information in this chapter and heaps more tips, hints and ideas for different kinds of parties in the book.

Putting on a successful party, of any kind or size, is not rocket science – it's all about getting organised. Start your preparation, whether it's a small supper for friends, a birthday barbecue, or a more formal event, as soon as you can. The less you leave to do at the last minute, the better.

Always throw a party that's right for you and within your capabilities. Don't be overambitious, or spend more than you really want to.

What kind of party?

You may have an idea of the kind of party you want to hold but don't make a final decision until you have considered several other important factors. Is your home big enough to hold that kind of party or will you need to hire a venue? How many guests are coming? What is your budget? How much time can you spend on preparation?

Where?

If you are holding the party at home, decide which rooms to use and what kinds of party would be best suited to what you have available. If you are planning to entertain outside remember to consider seating and what you will do if the weather lets you down. Always have a Plan B up your sleeve.

When?

The time of day you plan to hold your party will help you decide the kind of event and the food and drink to serve. Brunches, buffet lunches, barbecues, teas and picnics are ideal 'daytime' parties and for times when your guest list may include a wide diversity of ages.

How many?

This will be governed by the kind of event you are planning, the space you have available and your budget. If you are planning a sit-down meal you'll need to limit your numbers to the size of your dining table. You can cope with larger numbers by serving a buffet meal, or holding a drinks party or barbecue.

The budget?

Work out how much you want to spend. Entertaining doesn't have to be expensive but if you don't keep a tight rein on your budget from the start it can be. Start by making a list of everything you will need to buy. If you do this right at the beginning of your party planning you will quickly see where the money is going and there will be time to make adjustments. Being on a tight budget won't show if you choose food and wine carefully.

Budget for:

- Invitations
- Postage
- Flowers and decorations
- Food
- Drink
- Hiring anything you need – cutlery, china, equipment

Ways to keep control of the budget

- Prepare as much of the food as you can yourself.
- Select dishes that use foods that are in season – they'll be cheaper and full of flavour.
- Keep your food simple – you do not need to provide a wide range of choices.
- Serve wine and soft drinks not spirits.
- Keep your eyes open for special offers on wines. If you're buying a large amount ask for a discount or buy on 'sale or return'.
- Get your glasses on 'free hire' from the place you buy your wine.
- If you need extra serving dishes, an ice bucket, a punchbowl or a piece of kitchen equipment, ask around your friends. The chances are one of them will be happy to let you borrow theirs.

Invitations

Although it is now acceptable to phone or email invitations to all but the most formal events, everyone still likes to receive invitations in the post. If you telephone an invitation it's a good idea to follow it up with a short note.

Whether you phone or send an invitation remember to include:

- The kind of event. People like to know whether the party is to celebrate a special event, such as a birthday.
- Where it will be held. Include a map if necessary.
- The date and time.
- Whether there is a theme.
- What to wear. Guests really do like to know what to expect. It can be embarrassing to turn up in jeans and a shirt to be met by a hostess dressed as a flamenco dancer, with a matador, rose between his teeth, in tow!
- Make it clear whether children are invited. (A subtle way of raising this knotty problem if you're planning an adults-only event is to casually ask, 'Will you be all right getting a baby sitter?')
- Always ask guests to RSVP so you know how many are actually coming. It also gives you time to invite other people to make up the numbers if this is important. If guests are slow with their replies, give them a quick call.

- For all but the most impromptu parties, send out your invitations at least three weeks in advance to give prospective guests time to plan their schedules.
- Be specific about timings. If you are serving dinner at 8 p.m. invite guests for 7 p.m. so that there is plenty of time for 'stragglers' to arrive, and to serve apéritifs. If you need a party to end at a specific time don't be afraid to give a time on the invitation.

Remember to ask guests if there are any particular foods they cannot eat. It's generally easy to plan a meal around special dietary needs if you have advance warning.

The guest list

Don't get stressed drawing up your guest list – parties are meant to be enjoyable for you as well. Invite the people you want to have around you – but think about whether the event you are planning is the kind they will enjoy. For example, some people hate fancy dress but others can't wait to beat a path to the costume hire shop.

Themes?

Themes can give parties a sense of 'personality', are great icebreakers, and fun! Some parties lend themselves to themes, such as golden and silver wedding anniversaries, Halloween and Easter, but for other parties it's a case of putting on your thinking cap and devising something that suits the occasion. But it does take some effort to pull it off successfully and if you're not careful it can run away with the cash. Don't feel every party must have a theme.

Choose themes that are simple to create and whatever you do don't go overboard! Holding a black and white Roaring Twenties cocktail party and asking guests to dress accordingly is fine, using black and white china is fine, but trying to arrange for them to feast on black and white food at a black and white buffet table is way over the top!

Planning and preparation

This is where your lists are essential. Make separate lists of all the different aspects of party planning – guests, shopping, household tasks, items to be ordered – and keep them handy in a folder. The more you can get done in advance the more time you will have to devote to the personal touches that turn an average party into something memorable.

Food

Deciding on what to eat and drink may seem like negotiating a minefield. But relax. If you follow these general rules when deciding what to serve you can't go wrong:

* Reflect the impression given on your invitations. If the invitation says 'dinner' you will need two or three courses – a few bowls of crisps and nibbles won't fit the bill. Decide on a simple starter, a main course and a dessert. One or two courses are fine for an informal supper or lunch.
* Make sure that the dishes you choose can be eaten in the way you have planned. For example, if you are having an informal meal or buffet for a large group, with guests eating with their plates on their laps, select dishes that can easily be eaten with a fork.
* Choose dishes you know you do well.
* Decide on your main course first, or the principal dishes on a buffet, and then build the rest of the meal around it.
* If you are serving three courses choose a cold starter and/or dessert to cut down on cooking. Or choose dishes that can easily be reheated.
* Think about texture, colour and the presentation of your dishes.
* If you are short of time choose some dishes you can make or prepare in advance and freeze. Or buy some of the dishes.
* Be realistic about the time you can devote to cooking the food for your party. If necessary check out the deli and local caterers and order some of the food.
* Always buy the best-quality ingredients you can.
* Think of the space and facilities of your kitchen both for preparation and serving food on the day of the party.
* Don't serve too much food – you want your guests to feel comfortably satisfied not uncomfortably full!

Anthea's top tip

Presentation matters. When you've gone to a lot of trouble preparing food, don't waste the effort by plonking it on a plate. Remember, every dish is a feast for the eyes so think about garnishes, even if it is only a few mint leaves or a couple of sprigs of parsley.

How much to cook?

Per person:

Meat and poultry	4oz/100g
Fish (filleted)	6oz/175g
Prawns	6oz/175g
Rice or pasta (dry weight)	2oz/50g
Vegetables	6oz/175g
Fresh fruit	6oz/175g
Cream	3.5fl oz/100ml
Ice cream	7fl oz/200ml

Drinks

The days of providing your guests with a nonstop lake of wine and free-flowing spirits is long gone. Red and white wine, perhaps beer – depending on the occasion – and a selection of soft drinks and mineral water are all that is expected. Summer wine and fruit punches, and warm mulled wine on cold winter nights are always popular.

There's an awful lot of snobbery attached to wine, but don't worry about it. Choose wines you enjoy drinking or ask for suggestions from knowledgeable staff at wine merchants. It is fine to serve one wine throughout a dinner party, though you might like to finish with a sweet dessert wine.

How much to buy?

- For a dinner party allow three-quarters to one bottle of wine for each guest.
- For a drinks party allow half a bottle of wine per guest.
- For a daytime party allow one third of a bottle of wine for each guest.
- As a rough guide, and unless you're choosing to go with a particular type of food, buy two bottles of white wine to every bottle of red wine.

This is just a general guide, so it's a good idea to have a few bottles in reserve – you don't want to be rushing down to the all-night supermarket to replenish supplies halfway through the party!

TIPS

- Use picnic chiller boxes or large plastic bins filled with ice to chill wine, if you are short of fridge space.
- Make soft drinks interesting – decant them into attractive jugs and add fruity garnishes.
- If you are serving an iced fruit punch, freeze some of the fruit juice you are incorporating in ice-cube trays – then it won't dilute the punch.
- To get the maximum amount of juice from oranges, lemons and limes, roll the fruit under your hand on a flat surface before slicing in half and squeezing. Or pop them in the microwave for ten seconds before squeezing.
- Freeze clusters of grapes and hang them over the edge of your punchbowl.
- Freeze small pieces of lemon, lime, orange, or red berries in ice cubes, to drop into fresh juice drinks.
- If you are serving champagne, thoroughly rinse and dry the glasses. The merest trace of detergent will destroy the bubbles.

Want to learn more about wine?

See if an expert from your local wine merchant does home tasting sessions. Invite your friends round and arrange a wine tasting. All you will need to do is provide some savoury nibbles, olives and nuts. So there's another excuse to party!

Getting prepared

Well in advance:

* Plan your menu and make lists of all the food and drink you will need to buy or order. Get as much as you can delivered – it will save you valuable time.
* Check your table linen and napkins.
* Check crockery, cutlery and glassware and borrow or arrange to hire anything you need.
* Buy any decorations and invitations.
* Clean out the freezer to make room for dishes you can prepare ahead.
* Enlist help from friends and family, both to assist with preparation and on the day. Don't be a Mary Martyr – accept offers of help with open arms.

Three weeks to go:

* Send out your invitations.
* Make and freeze any dishes that can be prepared in advance.
* Buy in any non-perishable foods.
* Order your drinks (and glasses if you need them).
* Order flowers to be delivered the day before the party.
* Spring-clean the house.

Two days before:

* Do the remaining food shopping (if possible delay buying fresh vegetables and fruit until the day of the party).
* Prepare any food that can be prepared in advance.

The day before:

* Give the bathroom a good clean.
* Make a list of all the jobs to be done on the day of the party.
* Look around any rooms you plan to use, and remove any delicate ornaments in case they are accidentally broken.
* Arrange the flowers.

The day of the party:

- Lay the dining table or buffet table.
- Make sure there are ample clear surfaces for guests to put down their drinks. Lay out coasters and cover precious pieces of furniture with cloths to prevent them getting marked.
- Prepare the drinks table.
- Prepare the remaining food, leaving as little as possible to be done at the last minute.
- Set out all the serving dishes you will need and the coffee tray.
- Do a final check of the bathroom. Put out paper tissues, clean fluffy towels, luxurious soap and hand cream for your guests. Hide your cleaning products out of sight.
- Vacuum and tidy the rooms where the party will be held.
- Check that the hall and cloakroom area are clean and tidy. Remove all of the family's coats and put them out of the way if you are using the cloakroom for your guests' coats. If you are using a bedroom for coats make sure that it is clean and tidy.
- Aim to have all of your tasks completed at least an hour before your guests arrive so you have time to shower, dress and relax.

Anthea's top party tip

- Get the temperature right. You don't want your guests nodding off because it's too hot or dashing to get their coats for fear of frostbite!
- Whatever the occasion, try not to leave your guests unattended as soon as they arrive. Welcome them and make some introductions.
- A little well-chosen music will help set the mood – something soft and not overpowering. You want your guests to remember the scintillating conversation, not the booming beat (unless you are my husband!).

Be neighbourly

Warn your neighbours when you are having a party, particularly if it is likely to go on late, or invite them to join you. Also ask your guests not to block gateways and drives when they park their cars.

Setting the scene

Spend time setting the scene for your parties; your guests will certainly notice your efforts. It doesn't have to be expensive or time-consuming. Enhance your décor with a few carefully chosen flowers and a beautifully laid table to create the perfect party space. Remember, the simplest things often have the most effect.

Scene-setting tips

* Keep your flowers simple – a single colour with foliage looks incredibly chic. When you are buying flowers avoid large mixed bunches. Instead choose a few single blooms of one colour, or toning colours and some foliage.
* Keep dinner-table flower arrangements small, simple and low. A row of three bud vases all containing a single same-coloured rosebud or freesia always looks attractive. A centrepiece for a buffet table can be more extravagant – or you could use an arrangement of fruit and sprigs of foliage on a single-tiered cake stand.
* Overhead lights can be harsh. Think about changing the bulbs to a 'soft' light.
* Uplighters create a feeling of space.
* Use table lamps to illuminate dark areas.
* If you have dimmer switches use them to create the level of light that looks right for the occasion.
* If you are using candles keep a close eye on them and ensure they are placed away from anything flammable. Never leave candles unattended.
* Use unscented candles in the dining area as scented candles will mask the aroma of the food.

Anthea's top tip

Don't worry if all your china doesn't match. It doesn't have to. Just cover your table with a crisp white cloth, and it will set anything off beautifully

Setting the table

Be creative when it comes to setting your table, whether for dinner, supper, lunch or for a buffet – it's on display from the moment your guests arrive and helps to create the atmosphere.

Whether you choose to use a tablecloth or place mats is up to you. But if you are worried about spills or marks on your table it's wise to use a thick, waterproof table cover and a cloth when entertaining.

Think about whether you want to create an atmosphere that is formal, informal or thoroughly laid back. This will help you decide how to decorate your table. For example, if you are having a Mediterranean supper for friends, a bright tablecloth, coloured china and a small low bowl of lemons, limes and shiny bay leaves as a centrepiece could fit the bill. But if you are serving a more formal meal then a white tablecloth and napkins, sparkling glassware and a dainty arrangement of fresh flowers or candles will always create an air of sophistication. But don't be afraid to abandon convention and go for something different if you think it suits the occasion.

When to call in the experts

There may come a time when your home is not large enough for the party you are planning, so you'll need an alternative venue. Or you may decide that an event is too big, too grand, or you'd rather just hand over parts or the entire organisation to the professionals. That's fine – there's nothing wrong with delegation, however talented you are! And these days you can hire experts to do almost anything.

As a general rule the more formal and the larger an event, the more help you will need to make everything go like clockwork. Most hostesses will admit that arranging a 'do' for more than twenty guests is exhausting, particularly if you are planning to do all of the cooking. Don't believe anyone who tells you it takes no longer to prepare food for twenty than for six!

Hiring professionals is all about getting the right person for the job, whether it's a party planner to plan the whole event or hiring a couple of waitresses to serve the food. Some venues, such as hotels and conference centres, will be able to organise all of the catering for your party.

If you are hiring professionals or a venue do it as far ahead as you can – more than a year in advance in the case of a popular wedding location.

Here are some hints:

- Work out your budget – it is essential to know what you can spend.
- Shop around and do your research before hiring anyone. To find reliable party planners, caterers and other staff, ask around your friends, try to find out who organised or catered for an event you enjoyed, and check in the *Yellow Pages* and on the Internet to see who is available near you.
- Ensure the people you hire have a good track record and are experienced in the kind of event you are planning. Take up references and only hire people you feel comfortable with and who inspire you with confidence.
- Before you make a decision try to get detailed pricings from two or three companies. Make sure that the prices include any extras like transport costs, taxes, etc.
- Detail is everything, so get it in writing. You need to agree exactly what services they will be providing.
- Get a contract, and a receipt for any deposit you pay.
- Always give precise and detailed instructions and remember to keep a regular track on progress.
- Be guided by the experience of professionals but remember it is your party.
- If you are hiring a cook or caterer agree what they will cook, for how many, and where they will cook it. (For a small party you can hire a cook to come into your kitchen, cook up a feast, and then disappear as if by magic!) If the food isn't being cooked in your own kitchen visit their premises before hiring them.
- When you've decided on the menu ask for a tasting (you may be charged for this).
- If you need to hire waiting staff ask your caterer to recommend reliable people. Some caterers may have their own waiting staff.

When deciding on a venue, check the following:

- ✿ Does it have the atmosphere you want for your party?
- ✿ Does it have experience of the kind of event you are planning?
- ✿ Is there sufficient space, and all the facilities you need?
- ✿ Must you use the venue's caterers, staff and florists or can you hire your own?
- ✿ Is there access for disabled guests and are children allowed?
- ✿ Who will set up and clear the room?
- ✿ If you will be taking photographs is there a suitable setting?
- ✿ What time will you be allowed in and what time will you have to leave?
- ✿ Is there an area where you can greet your guests or where pre-dinner drinks can be served?
- ✿ Is there sufficient car parking?

Now let's party. In the following chapters you'll find all you need to know to make every party you ever give a sparkling success.

CHAPTER 2
BREAKFASTS, BRUNCHES AND COFFEE MORNINGS

Leisurely weekend breakfasts, brunch parties and smart coffee mornings are a style of easy entertaining that's simple to plan and prepare. The beauty of breakfast and brunch parties is that you can produce a sumptuous spread without spending hours in the kitchen or breaking the bank.

You don't need a reason for this kind of entertaining, but it's an ideal way to celebrate weekend birthdays, to get together with friends and family, or perhaps as a prelude to an afternoon visit to a stately home, sporting event, carnival or fête. Coffee mornings are a great opportunity to indulge your guests – and yourself – with delicious coffee and naughty-but-nice cakes and pastries.

Before you rush off to plan a menu for a breakfast or brunch, decide how many guests to invite. The number will depend on whether everyone will be sitting around the dining table or kitchen table or whether you are planning a buffet-style feast with guests serving themselves from a table or sideboard and eating with their plates on their laps. Summertime breakfasts and brunches in the garden are a real treat.

BREAKFASTS

With some creative shopping at the supermarket, deli and baker's, breakfasts can involve little or even no cooking. You could serve a no-cook continental-style breakfast or alternatively your own variation of the traditional British breakfast. Add freshly brewed tea and coffee and glasses of chilled buck's fizz for an unforgettable lazy-day feast.

For a stylish continental breakfast you could serve:

- An exotic breakfast fruit salad – orange segments, pink grapefruit, mango and cantaloupe melon. Accompany the fruit with a bowl of Greek yogurt drizzled with a little honey or maple syrup and a bowl of crunchy granola. (In the winter serve a warm compote of dried fruit with a touch of cinnamon. Steep the fruit in cold tea for several hours before cooking.)
- Platters of cold and cured meats (try some of the more unusual continental meats) garnished with tomato wedges and parsley.
- Platters of thin slices of cheese such as Gruyère, Emmenthal and Jarlsberg, and small chunks of Gouda, Edam or feta – ask the assistants at your deli counter to suggest any other Continental cheeses that can be sliced. Finish the platters with quarters of hard-boiled egg, cocktail gherkins and black olives.
- Baskets of warmed breakfast breads such as croissants, baguettes, crusty rolls, brioche and walnut bread (delicious with cheese and cold meats). Remember the butter and conserves.
- Pains au chocolat and small Danish pastries.
- Hot chocolate, coffee, tea, chilled fruit juice and mineral water.

For a traditional English breakfast you could serve:

- A seasonal fresh fruit salad or a winter fruit salad with a bowl of yogurt.
- A bowl of fresh fruit – kiwi fruit, pears, figs, apples and bananas.
- Cereals and luxury muesli.
- Breakfast muffins.
- English breakfast favourites – eggs, bacon, sausages, baked diced potato, mushrooms, smoked salmon, kippers, omelettes.
- Smoked haddock with poached eggs.
- Crusty rolls and bread, with butter, marmalade, jam and honey.
- Toast, crumpets, English muffins or Scotch pancakes.
- Coffee, tea, hot chocolate, chilled fruit juice and mineral water.

Buck's fizz
(Serves 10)

750ml bottle of chilled champagne or sparkling wine
10 oranges, juiced

Fill the glasses one third full with orange juice and top up with champagne. Serve immediately.

BRUNCH PARTIES

If it's too late for breakfast and too early for lunch – then it's time for brunch. Brunch parties usually begin between 11 a.m. and noon.

You can serve the same dishes as you would for breakfast, but you may also want to add other hot and cold dishes, depending on the number of guests. Keep the dishes simple, and choose dishes that can be served cold or made in advance and reheated.

Here are some ideas to add to the brunch buffet table:

* The New York deli favourite, bagels with cream cheese and smoked salmon. Make them in advance or place a basket of bagels on a large platter with a bowl of cream cheese and a plate of smoked salmon.
* A baked gammon.
* A seafood platter.
* American-style pancake stacks with maple syrup and crispy bacon.
* Crunchy French bread mini pizzas.
* Devilled kidneys on French bread croutes.
* Griddled tomato on toasted ciabatta.
* Bruschetta with an assortment of toppings.
* A spicy kedgeree.

Devilled kidneys

(Serves 8)

2 baguettes cut into thin slices
Olive oil
75g/3oz butter and 1tbsp olive oil
3 cloves garlic, crushed
2 shallots, finely chopped
225g/8oz button mushrooms, halved
3tbsp Worcestershire sauce
½tsp cayenne pepper
16 lambs' kidneys, halved and trimmed
300ml/½ pint double cream
1tbsp roughly chopped parsley

1. Preheat the oven to 160°C/Gas 3.
2. Brush the baguette slices with oil. Place on a baking tray and bake in the oven until golden. (These can be baked in advance and reheated.)
3. Melt the butter in the pan with the tablespoon of olive oil. Add the garlic, shallots and mushrooms and cook gently until the shallots have softened. Add the Worcestershire sauce and cayenne pepper and cook for a further minute. Cut each of the kidney halves in half again. Add to the pan and simmer until they are cooked through, stirring occasionally.
4. Stir in the cream and simmer for 2 minutes until the sauce has thickened slightly.
5. Arrange the warmed bread slices around a serving plate and place the devilled kidneys in the centre. Garnish with the parsley.

Spicy kedgeree
(Serves 4–6)

700g/1½ lbs smoked haddock, skin and any bones removed
1 onion, finely chopped
1 heaped tsp hot curry powder
225g/8oz long grain rice (dry weight)
450ml/16fl oz of the fish cooking liquid
50g/2oz butter
1 tbsp olive oil
3 hard-boiled eggs, shelled and chopped
100g/4oz frozen peas, cooked
2 tbsp parsley
To garnish:
1 tbsp fresh parsley, chopped
1 hard-boiled egg, cut into wedges
Lemon wedges

1. Place the fish in a large saucepan and cover with 570ml/1 pint of water. Bring to the boil, reduce the heat and simmer for 6–8 minutes until the fish is cooked. Drain off the water into a measuring jug and keep to use later. Place the fish on a plate, cover with foil and keep warm.
2. Melt the butter and oil in the saucepan and add the chopped onion. Gently cook until the onion has softened. Add the curry powder and cook for a further minute. Add the rice and 450ml/16fl oz of the reserved liquid. Stir together and bring to the boil. Cover the saucepan with a lid and simmer very gently for 10 minutes.
3. When the rice has been cooking for 10 minutes, flake the fish and lay it on top of the rice. Add the frozen peas, half of the parsley, and three chopped hard-boiled eggs. Do not stir it into the rice. Allow the rice to continue cooking for another 8 minutes or until it is cooked, by which time the water will have been absorbed.
4. Remove from the heat and gently stir the fish, peas, hard-boiled egg and parsley into the rice and onions. At this stage you can add another 25g/1oz of butter or 3 tablespoons of single cream into the kedgeree to make a richer dish. Transfer to a warmed serving dish. Garnish with lemon wedges, hard-boiled egg wedges and a tablespoon of parsley.

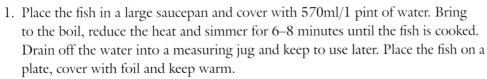

BREAKFAST AND BRUNCH TIPS

❁ If you are feeding a crowd give fried eggs a miss – they need to be cooked and eaten quickly. Instead prepare creamy scrambled eggs. Serve plain or add strips of smoked salmon or cooked prawns.

❁ Serve chilled fruit juice in jugs, not out of the boxes or bottles.

❁ If you are serving cereals and muesli buy individual packets or sachets so the family doesn't have several half-empty packets to plough their way through afterwards.

❁ Buy a couple of small unglazed ceramic tiles from the DIY shop, warm them in the oven and place under linen napkins in breadbaskets to keep rolls warm. You can also buy bread-warming tiles from homeware shops.

❁ Use food warmers to keep food hot on the buffet table – but make sure they are placed where children cannot reach them.

Mother's Day breakfast

Let your children plan breakfast in bed, or a special family breakfast, on Mother's Day.

If you opt for breakfast in bed let them plan the menu, do the shopping and prepare a beautiful breakfast tray with a tiny posy of flowers. Always have an adult on hand to supervise.

They could serve a small fresh fruit salad, warmed croissants and marmalade, with tea or coffee – or maybe mini Danish pastries, and steaming hot chocolate. To give the day a real sense of occasion serve buck's fizz – use a miniature bottle of champagne and the freshly squeezed juice of an orange.

Or start the day with a special champagne family breakfast. Let the children make all the arrangements – shopping, laying the table and serving the food – if they are old enough. If they want to make a cooked breakfast be ready to lend a hand and offer suggestions. They could serve fresh fruit, cereals and yogurt followed by simple scrambled egg on toast accompanied by croissants and marmalade. Stacks of American pancakes drizzled with maple syrup and accompanied by crisp bacon are a popular alternative – especially with the children. Don't forget a junior version of buck's fizz made with fresh orange juice and lemonade.

Mother's Day is also a lovely excuse to get the extended family together and treat all the 'mums' in the group. So why not throw a Mother's Day brunch?

Father's Day breakfast

Let the children give Dad some special treatment on Father's Day with a buck's fizz breakfast or brunch followed by a boy's day out – a session on a dry ski slope, a spin at a race track, a paintball adventure or a hot-air balloon ride. Or plan a family day out at a local beauty spot or attraction.

Easter brunch

After the dark days of winter, by the time spring arrives most people are ready to party. So it's a great time to decorate the house with spring flowers and get everyone round for an informal brunch party. Devise an Easter egg hunt, an egg-rolling race or an Easter bonnet parade to keep the children happy.

For an Easter egg hunt:

- Work out the route for the hunt (if the weather's fine you could use the garden) on paper first and then prepare a series of clues to lead to the 'treasure'. If the hunt is inside it's a good idea to close all rooms that are out of bounds and explain that clues are only in rooms that have the doors open. (In the interests of safety avoid clues in the kitchen, please. If the treasure hunt is held in the garden remember to check that garden ponds, garages and swimming pools are covered or closed off. Ensure that garden boundaries are secure and any gates firmly closed.)
- You might like to hide a cache of miniature eggs with each clue so that the children can each remove one when they discover the clue. Give each of the children a pretty bag to collect their eggs.
- If the treasure is too big to hide easily, let the final clue lead them to a person at the party who can produce the prize. If you don't, the chances are that an eagle-eyed little one will spot the prize two minutes into the hunt!
- Attach a scroll from the Easter bunny to a door explaining what the children have to do to reach the treasure – then they can always pop back to refresh their memories.
- If you have several small children at the party it might be an idea to have a simpler Easter egg hunt confined to one room just for them. They could simply hunt out hidden eggs, without the need for clues.

More Easter games

- If the weather is fine have an egg-and-spoon race.
- Hold an Easter bonnet parade (it'll give the children, and mums and dads of course, a chance to have some messy fun in the days before the party).
- Stage a painted (hard-boiled) egg exhibition and ask the children and adults to submit their masterpieces for display. (You'll need to collect a heap of egg cups – or ask guests to bring their exhibits in egg cups.)
- Have an egg-rolling competition if it's dry. The eggs could be rolled using noses to a finishing line, or you could set up a slalom course and let each runner push their egg round the course with a length of dowelling – you'd need someone to stand by with a stopwatch.
- Remember to have a stock of inexpensive prizes handy.

Easter egg nests

Children will love making these Easter egg nests for a party.
(Makes 12)

50g/2oz butter
100g/4oz good quality milk chocolate, broken into small pieces
3tbsp golden syrup
2tbsp cocoa
100g/4oz puffed rice cereal
14 small paper cake cases
To decorate:
Mini sugar coated chocolate eggs

1. Place the chocolate, cocoa, butter and syrup into a large saucepan. Heat gently, stirring all the time until the chocolate has melted and the mixture is well combined.
2. Remove the pan from the heat and add the puffed rice cereal. Stir gently until the cereal is coated with the chocolate mixture.
3. Place the cake cases in a bun tray and spoon in the mixture. Using a teaspoon make a dent in the centre of each to form a nest shape. Place three sugar coated eggs in the hollow. Leave to set.

COFFEE MORNINGS

Coffee mornings are a lovely way to catch up with girlfriends. Get the children off to school or nursery, and the chores done, then invite them round for 'elevenses'. (If you have friends with tinies, persuade them to get a babysitter for a couple of hours, so they can come along and relax.)

Make it an occasion. Give your coffee mornings the whole 'coffee shop' treatment with frothy coffee and delicious cakes and cookies. You only need two or three kinds of cakes – preferably small and home-made – and some biscuits or biscotti. So get out your cookery books and create a sweet treat – chocolate, coffee, almond and nutty flavours go particularly well with coffee.

A good read

Why not exercise your mind as well as your mouth by combining your coffee morning with a book group? Let friends take it in turns to choose a book to read and then discuss it the following month. Take it in turns to host the group. (Some bookshops will give you a discount when you buy books for a book group, so it's worth checking whether your local shop has a scheme.)

If your friends are working during the day, you could make it an evening book group and serve wine and simple nibbles. Or combine a coffee morning or evening get-together with a clothes swap or a book exchange.

Here are some of my top reads:

- *The Kite Runner* (Khaled Hosseini)
- *Behind the Scenes at the Museum* (Kate Atkinson)
- *The Shadow of the Wind* (Carlos Ruiz Zafon)
- *The No. 1 Ladies' Detective Agency* (Alexander McCall Smith)
- *Skipping Christmas* (John Grisham)
- *The Secret* (Rhonda Byrne) – the only self-help book I recommend!

Coffee-morning specials

Anthea's polo cake
(Makes 12 pieces)

4 eggs
250g/9oz soft margarine
250g /9oz caster sugar
350g/12oz self-raising flour
4tbsp milk
350g/12oz sultanas
50g/2oz glacé cherries, chopped
2tbsp demerara sugar

1. Preheat the oven to 180°C/Gas 4. Line a deep-sided swiss roll tin with baking parchment.
2. Place the margarine, caster sugar, eggs and flour in a large bowl and beat for 2 minutes with an electric beater. Beat in the milk. Stir in the sultanas and cherries.
3. Spoon the mixture into your prepared tin and bake in the oven for 30 to 35 minutes until the top is golden and firm.
4. Allow to cool and cut into small squares or fingers.

Coffee squares
(Makes about 20)

175g/6oz caster sugar
175g/6oz soft margarine
1tbsp instant coffee, dissolved in 1tbsp boiling water, allowed to cool
75g/3oz chopped walnuts
175g/6oz self-raising flour
1tsp baking powder
3 large eggs
For the icing:
225g/8oz icing sugar, sieved
75g/3oz soft margarine
1tbsp milk

1tbsp instant coffee, dissolved in 1tbsp boiling water
Chopped walnuts to decorate

1. Heat the oven to 160˚C/Gas 3. Grease and line a 30x22.5cm (12x9-inch) straight-sided baking tin.
2. Place the margarine, sugar and coffee dissolved in water in a bowl and beat until well blended and smooth. Lightly beat the eggs and add to the mixture. Stir in the walnuts. Beat in the flour and baking powder until the mixture is smooth.
3. Turn into the prepared baking tin and cook for 40 – 45 minutes until the cake is firm and well risen and has begun to shrink away from the sides. Leave to cool in the tin before turning out onto a rack.
4. To make the icing combine the icing sugar, the dissolved coffee, margarine and milk into a bowl and beat until smooth. Spread over the cake and sprinkle with the walnuts. When the icing has set cut into small squares.

Orange cookies
(Makes 20)

100g/4oz caster sugar
100g/4oz butter, softened
1 medium egg yolk
Grated rind of 1 orange
1tbsp orange juice
175g/6oz plain flour
1 level tsp baking powder

1. Preheat the oven to 180˚C/Gas 4.
2. Place the caster sugar and butter in a mixing bowl and beat until creamy. Add the egg yolk, orange rind and orange juice and mix together. Add the flour and baking powder and mix together until a stiff dough is formed. Knead lightly with your fingers until the dough leaves the bowl clean. Form into a ball, wrap in clingfilm and chill in the fridge for an hour.
3. Divide the mixture into 20 small balls. Place them on baking sheets lined with nonstick baking parchment and flatten. Bake for 10 to 15 minutes until they are pale golden brown. Leave to cool for 5 minutes then lift onto a cooling rack. Store in an airtight tin when they are completely cold.

CHAPTER 3
LUNCHES AND TEAS

If you enjoy relaxed entertaining then laid-back lunches and afternoon tea parties are the perfect choice for you. Most of us have a few never-fail, simple, light dishes we can produce at the drop of the hat – and that's all you need. And when it comes to afternoon tea it's a chance to indulge your guest (and yourself) with dainty sandwiches and a delicious array of cakes.

LUNCHES

Weekends and holidays are the most popular times for lunch parties, so aim for an informal atmosphere. Lunches – unless they are of the traditional 'Sunday roast' variety – usually involve serving light dishes. A round-the-table lunch is often simplest when you are entertaining a few guests, but for more than about eight, a buffet-style meal fits the bill perfectly.

Two well-chosen courses are all you need – perhaps with the addition of a cheeseboard, grapes and maybe some fresh figs. Whether you choose to serve a soup or starter followed by a main course, or a main course and a dessert, is entirely up to you. On cold winter days a lunch of a chunky home-made soup with chunks of warm crusty bread followed by an apple tart, a fruit crumble or a creamy bread-and-butter pudding will go down a treat with even the most discerning guests.

If you opt for a starter, how about bruschetta or a light soup with warm crusty bread? A simple dish of grilled, pan-fried or baked fish, meat or chicken with seasonal vegetables makes an ideal main course for small groups. Main-meal salads, risottos or light pasta dishes accompanied by a salad are also quick and easy to produce. Finish with a delicate fruit dessert or a more substantial dessert if your main course is particularly light.

If the numbers are larger save time in the kitchen by choosing some dishes that can be prepared in advance and served cold or reheated. Try dishes such as a pasta bake, savoury tarts, Spanish tortillas and cold meats, accompanied by a selection of salads.

❧ Lunch menu for 8 ❧
(Serve either a starter or a dessert)

Roasted pepper and tomato bruschetta

———

Citrus and chilli salmon on a bed of watercress
Boiled new potatoes
Beans and asparagus

———

Ginger baked peaches with fresh raspberry sauce and fromage frais

❧ Lunch menu for 20 ❧
(Serve either a starter or a dessert)

Tapas

———

French onion tart
Spanish mushroom tortilla
Spicy chicken kebabs
A lasagne
A platter of cold meats
Herby new potatoes
A selection of salads

———

Lemon cheesecake
Red berry fruit salad with rosewater cream

———

Cheese and biscuits

Roasted pepper and tomato bruschetta
(Makes 12 slices)

1 ciabatta loaf, cut into slices
1 jar roasted red peppers
1 jar roasted sun-dried tomatoes in oil
12 stuffed black olives (optional)

1. Preheat the oven to 180°C/Gas 4.
2. Decant a little of the oil from the jar of roasted sun dried tomatoes and use to brush one side of each of the slices of bread. Slice the roasted red peppers and the roasted sun-dried tomatoes and arrange on the slices of bread. Slice the stuffed olives and scatter over. Bake in the preheated oven for 12–15 minutes until the vegetables are hot and the bread crisp.

Citrus and chilli salmon
(Serves 8)

Juice of a lime
6tbsp clear sweet chilli sauce
Olive oil (to wipe the pan)
8 salmon steaks, skin removed
2tsp water
200g bag of ready-prepared watercress
Freshly ground black pepper to serve

1. Combine the sweet chilli sauce with the lime juice.
2. Wipe a large nonstick frying pan with olive oil and heat gently. Add the salmon steaks and cook for 3 minutes. Turn the fish over and cook for 2 minutes, then add the sauce and the water to the pan and continue cooking until the salmon is cooked through. Don't overcook the salmon or it will be dry.
3. Arrange the watercress on a serving plate and place the salmon on the top.

Ginger baked peaches

(Serves 8)

8 ripe peaches
20 ginger crunch or ginger nut biscuits, roughly crushed
50g/2oz butter, melted
2tbsp runny honey
2tbsp dark rum (optional)
Juice of 2 small oranges

1. Preheat the oven to 180°C/Gas 4.
2. Cut the nectarines or peaches in half and remove the stones.
3. Combine the crushed biscuits, melted butter, honey and rum, if using, and fill the centres of the peaches or nectarines, from where the stone has been removed.
4. Place the fruit into an ovenproof baking dish. Pour over the orange juice, taking care not to dislodge the filling. Bake for 15 – 20 minutes.
5. Serve with whipped cream or Greek yogurt.

Traditional Sunday lunch

The traditional Sunday roast lunch is a meal to be savoured, and the hostess who is happy to take on the challenge will have guests beating a path to her door. It may seem difficult but it's all a matter of selecting dishes which you feel confident cooking and getting the timing right.

It's wise to decide on a menu and then work out a timetable of when things need to be done. Start from the time you want to have the meal on the table and work backwards.

Choose a cold or prepare-ahead starter if you are serving one – though it's not essential – and a dessert that can be reheated or served cold. Then you can concentrate all your efforts on the day on the main course. Instead of a starter you might like to serve a tray of canapés and nibbles with a pre-lunch drink.

If you are serving a starter keep it simple – such as chilled melon and grapefruit cocktail or smoked salmon with dainty triangles of wholemeal bread and wedges of lemon.

Unless you are an experienced 'Sunday roaster', a succulent leg of English lamb is probably a safe bet – beef can easily end up too well done or too rare. The timing of a perfectly cooked large chicken can be difficult to gauge, and if it takes longer than expected will mess up your carefully calculated timings.

For dessert settle for individual cold creations or, in winter, a traditional apple pie (made the day before and reheated) with cream or ice cream, a special fruit crumble or a sticky toffee pudding. If you are short of time buy a dessert from one of the luxury ranges at the supermarket or deli.

Presentation is the key. Make sure that all the rooms your guests will see are spotless and inviting. Pay attention to the appearance of your table and its decorations, whether you decide on crisp white linen or something more rustic.

Prepare everything you can on the day before the party. Lay the table, prepare a tray for coffee and get out any serving dishes you plan to use.

❧ Sunday lunch menu ❧

Roast leg of lamb with a rosemary and redcurrant crumb crust
Seasonal vegetables
Roast parsnips
Roast potatoes
Red wine gravy
Mint sauce

Spicy apple pie and cream

Roast leg of lamb with a rosemary and redcurrant crumb crust
(This quantity is sufficient for a whole leg of lamb. If you are using a ½ leg of lamb, make half the quantity of crust.)

1 leg of lamb joint
3 slices of wholemeal bread, crumbed
3 tbsp redcurrant jelly
5 sprigs of rosemary, chopped
2 tsp olive oil
1 garlic clove, crushed

1. Place the redcurrant jelly, olive oil and crushed garlic clove into a bowl and mix together. Add the breadcrumbs and the chopped rosemary and mix again. Press the crust onto the outside of the lamb joint and roast for the required time. The roasting time will depend on the size of the joint.

Spicy apple pie
(Serves 6)

350g/12oz ready-to-use shortcrust pastry
450g/1½lb cooking apples, peeled, cored and thickly sliced
75g/3oz light soft brown sugar
½ tsp cinnamon
50g/2oz sultanas (optional)
2 level tbsp cornflour
Milk and a little demerara (or granulated) sugar to glaze

1. Preheat the oven to 200°C/Gas 6.
2. Take just over half of the pastry and roll out so that it is large enough to line the base and sides of a 23cm/9 inch loose-bottomed, straight-sided or fluted metal flan dish – do not cut off any pastry which is over the edge of the dish at this stage.
3. Place the thick slices of apple in a large bowl and add the light soft brown sugar, cinnamon and sultanas, if used. Stir to mix together. Sprinkle over the cornflour and mix again. Place the apple mixture into the pastry-lined dish.
4. Roll out the remaining pastry so that it is a little larger than the top of the dish. Place over the dish. Run a rolling pin over the edges of the dish to seal the edge and remove the excess pastry. Roll out the trimmings to make leaf shapes and use these to decorate the top of the pie. Brush the top with milk and sprinkle with demerara sugar.
5. Bake the pie in the oven for 20 minutes, then reduce the heat of the oven to 160°C/Gas 4 and cook for a further 15–20 minutes until the pastry is golden. If the pie begins to brown too quickly simply lay a piece of greaseproof paper across the top to deflect the heat.
6. Serve with pouring cream or vanilla ice cream.

I usually skip the starter when I'm doing Sunday lunch and let everyone get straight into the main event – as most people want to come back for 'seconds'. When I'm serving lamb I like it studded with rosemary and garlic slivers. And I can't resist Yorkshire puddings so I serve them whatever the meat!

The secret of a successful Sunday lunch is getting as much done in advance as you can possibly can. You can even cook the roast potatoes the night before. All you have to do is parboil the potatoes, drain and dust with a little flour. Tip them into a baking tray, drizzle with oil and bake in the normal way until crisp. Then let them cool completely and cover the tray with a piece of foil. All you have to do next day is whack them into the oven for the last fifteen minutes before lunch is served and you'll have delicious crispy roast potatoes every time.

I also like to serve a tray of roasted root vegetables – parsnips, swede, carrots and turnip. All you do is put chunks of the vegetables into a baking tray with a quartered red onion, a few cloves of garlic and a bay leaf. Drizzle with oil and bake in a moderate oven until they are tender.

Girly Indulgence Day

Have a 'Girly Indulgence Day' for your friends and serve a light lunch. Persuade beauty-therapist friends (or hire some) to come along to give your guests a manicure, a pedicure, a relaxing reflexology session or a massage. (You could turn this into a fundraiser for your favourite charity by asking your friends to make a donation in exchange for their pampering.)

Or you could hold an evening pampering session and serve a simple fork supper.

Anthea's top tip

At a really successful girly day I held, we had highlights in the kitchen, massage in the bedroom and reflexology on the sofa while the rest of us sat around gossiping, watching re-runs of *Charlie's Angels*, reading magazines and munching Minstrels and M&S Percy Pigs. It was so easy, so relaxing and fun.

AFTERNOON TEA PARTIES

It's a great pity that we don't get more invitations to tea parties. Afternoon tea is a wonderful meal – when else do you get a chance to eat fresh scones topped with cream and jam, crumpets dripping with butter, dainty sandwiches and a real home-baked Victoria sandwich cake? And what could be nicer than sitting around a roaring log fire in winter having tea with a group of friends or the family?

Tea parties are also a perfect way to entertain larger numbers – particularly in summer when you can use the garden. Give a tea party to celebrate birthdays, anniversaries . . . or for no special reason at all.

Again, whether you are entertaining a small group or a crowd, getting the preparation right is the key to success. Decide what you are going to serve, how many guests to invite and where the party will be held, and then it's plain sailing.

Let's take it as read that your house will be uncluttered, clean and sparkling when your guests arrive. Arrange fresh flowers in the rooms you will be using. If you plan to hold your party outside, give the garden a tidy and set out tables and chairs. (If you haven't got enough have some blankets and cushions handy so that guests can sit on the lawn.)

Make your serving table look beautiful with a white linen or damask tablecloth and a small arrangement of fresh flowers.

The food

Aim for daintiness as far as the food is concerned. Serve three or four different kinds of sandwiches, a selection of cakes, and small scones. Savoury items such as small savoury tartlets or sausage rolls (preferably home-made) are always well received – particularly by male guests!

Teatime sandwiches should be made with thin slices of bread, and the fillings tasty but not deep-filled. This is one occasion when buying a pile of door-step sandwiches from the supermarket and cutting them in half just won't do! Keep sandwiches cool and covered with clingfilm until they are needed.

TIPS FOR SUCCESSFUL SANDWICHES

● Use bread that is a day old and softened butter so that you can spread it evenly – right to the corners.

● Make sure your fillings are firm and do not soak into the sandwiches or leak out.

● Cut off the crusts as you make each round of sandwiches – they will be neater than if you try to cut through a stack.

Try these fillings:

● Red salmon mashed with a little mayonnaise seasoned with freshly ground black pepper and a squeeze of lemon juice, topped with finely cut cucumber slices.

● Mashed hard-boiled egg and cress mixed with a little natural fromage frais and mayonnaise, seasoned with salt and freshly ground black pepper.

● Thin-sliced cucumber seasoned with salt and pepper and a touch of vinegar.

● Finely sliced rare roast beef, lightly spread with horseradish sauce.

● Soft cream cheese combined with finely grated mature Cheddar and some finely chopped chives.

● Finely sliced chicken or turkey lightly spread with cranberry jelly and seasoned with salt and pepper.

Try to bake your own cakes – or persuade a keen cake-maker among your friends to make some for you. Steer clear of six-inch-high creamy gateaux but settle instead for small cakes, and beautifully decorated sponges and tea breads. With a little clever shopping it is possible to include some shop-bought items, but give the kind of everyday slices and cakes that your guests will recognise instantly a miss.

Reserve crumpets and teacakes for occasions when you only have a few guests, as these are best served straight from the toaster.

The drinks

Serve a good-quality tea, and some soft drinks or coffee for those who don't drink tea. Provide milk jugs and sugar bowls beside the teacups, and have a dish of lemon slices for anyone who prefers to drink their tea black. If it's a summer party try serving a cooling iced tea punch.

Iced tea punch
(Serves 20)

20 tea bags
10 glasses of water (of the size you plan to use)
15tsp caster sugar
250ml/9fl oz unsweetened pineapple juice
250ml/9fl oz pint fresh orange juice
Juice of 2 limes
1 litre ginger ale

Boil the water and make the tea in the usual way. Stir in the sugar and allow the tea to get cold. Then pour in the remaining ingredients and stir well. Taste and add more sugar if necessary. Chill until ready to serve. Garnish with orange and lime slices. Serve in straight-sided glasses with or without ice.

Off the shelf

- Buy plain ready-made fairy cakes and decorate them yourself.
- Buy a luxury Madeira cake, remove it from its case and drizzle over a lemon-flavoured glacé icing. Or flavour your icing with a little rose water and arrange sugared rose petals on the top.
- Buy a lemon loaf cake. Place the juice of half a large lemon and two tablespoons of caster sugar in a saucepan and bring to the boil, stirring all the time. Allow the syrup to cool slightly and then pour over the cake. Serve as it is or top with glacé icing – allow the icing to drip over the sides of the cake. Decorate with sugared orange or lemon slices.

- Look out for luxury thick shortbread rounds and interesting 'home-baked' style biscuits – arrange them on a plate with some genuine home-made biscuits and no one will notice.
- To save time buy icings and frostings at the supermarket to decorate your cakes.
- If you don't feel confident baking from scratch, buy luxury cake mixes from the supermarket. They are very reliable and simple to make and decorate.
- Decorate a plain Victoria sandwich in a flash by placing a craft stencil on top of the cake and then dusting with icing sugar.
- Many cakes and sponges freeze well, and then all you have to do is defrost and decorate them the day before the party.
- Women's Institute markets, farm shops, fine food outlets and some local delis are great places to find home-made cakes on sale, both ready-iced and plain for you to decorate at home.
- Buy an un-iced home-made-style fruitcake. Brush the top with melted apricot jam and arrange walnut halves and glazed cherries around the edge or over the entire top of the cake. Brush the walnuts and cherries with more apricot jam.

- Use cocktail-sized sweet shortcrust tartlet cases to make jam or lemon curd tarts. Spoon a teaspoon of warmed jam or lemon curd into the cases. As the jam or lemon curd cools it will set.

TEATIME TIPS

- Serve cakes that are small and not too fragile – if they can be picked up with fingers you won't need cake forks.
- To prevent cloths blowing off tables in the garden sew triangular pockets at the corners and slip curtain weights or flat pebbles into the pockets.
- If you have a large number of guests borrow teapots from friends or hire them. It's so much nicer than making tea in an urn!
- Enlist the help of a friend as assistant tea maker, so you don't have to keep rushing away from your guests to refill teapots.
- Make sure you have enough teaspoons.
- Look out for large white linen tablecloths in charity shops and antique markets – you can often pick up beautiful tablecloths from a bygone era at very reasonable prices.

Sugared cake decorations

Sugared edible flowers make an attractive decoration for cakes. They are simple to make, and will certainly impress your guests.

These are some edible flowers:

- Rose
- Violet
- Pansy
- Nasturtium
- Geranium
- Primrose

Carefully wash the flower heads and allow to dry. Roses need to be separated into petals and sugared individually.

Break an egg white into a small bowl and, using an artist's paintbrush, paint the egg white onto the petals or flower heads. Sprinkle with caster sugar. Place on a baking sheet lined with baking parchment and allow to dry in a warm place. This will take about 24 hours.

Herbs such as mint, rosemary and sage can also be sugared in the same way.

Small bunches of grapes can be sugared, too. Simply dip small bunches of them in egg white, shake off any excess and sprinkle with caster sugar. Leave to dry.

Note: not all flowers are edible. If you are not sure or cannot identify a flower, do not eat it.

Mocha sponge sandwich
(Makes 10 slices)

175g/6oz soft margarine
175g/6oz caster sugar
175g/6oz self-raising flour
1½tsp baking powder
3 medium eggs
1tbsp instant coffee dissolved in 1tbsp boiling water
1tbsp cocoa
1tbsp milk
For the filling and topping:
225g/8oz icing sugar, sifted
100g/4oz butter, softened
1tbsp instant coffee dissolved in 1tbsp boiling water
40g/1½oz drinking chocolate
1tsp milk
Chocolate coffee beans, to decorate

1. Preheat the oven to 180°C/Gas 4. Grease and line the base of 2 x 20cm (8-inch) sponge tins.
2. Place all of the cake ingredients into a mixing bowl and beat with an electric mixer for 2 to 3 minutes until well blended.
3. Divide the mixture between the prepared tins and bake for 35 to 40 minutes until the cakes are well risen and firm to the touch. Turn out onto wire racks and remove the lining paper. Allow to cool completely.
4. To make the filling and topping put all of the remaining ingredients into a bowl and beat until smooth. If the icing appears too stiff add another teaspoon of milk.
5. Place the sponges on top of each other with the flat bases of the cakes together. Remove one of the sponges and cover the bottom sponge with half of the icing. Replace the second sponge, and press lightly. Cover with the remaining icing. Create a swirl pattern with the back of a spoon or fork. Decorate with chocolate coffee beans.

* Make 20 slices of cake for your tea party by simply icing the tops of each of the sponges. Decorate one with chocolate coffee beans and the other with dark-chocolate buttons or ready-made chocolate leaves (you'll find them in the baking aisle at the supermarket).

Almond and lemon cake
(Makes 2 cakes)

A handful of slivered almonds
225g/8oz caster sugar
225g/8oz soft margarine
4 medium eggs
225g/8oz self-raising flour, sifted
Grated rind of ½ lemon
For the topping:
75g/3oz granulated sugar
Juice of 1 lemon

1. Preheat the oven to 160°C/Gas 3. Grease and line two 17.5cm (7-inch) round loose-bottomed cake tins. Scatter the slivered almonds over the bases.
2. Place the sugar and margarine in a mixing bowl and beat until the mixture is pale and fluffy. Beat in the eggs, one at a time, beating well after the addition of each egg. Beat in the lemon zest and fold in the flour with a spoon. Transfer half of the mixture into each of the cake tins and bake for 45 minutes or until a skewer comes out clean. Remove from the oven.
3. Leave to cool for 5 minutes then turn the cakes onto a wire cooling rack so that the slivered almonds are on the top surface. Combine the granulated sugar and the lemon juice in a small bowl and mix well. Spoon over the cakes immediately and allow to cool completely. Just before serving cut into slices.

Chocolate rum truffle cake
(Makes 12 squares)

675g/1½lb plain cake (Madeira or similar), crumbled
50g/2oz walnuts, chopped
50g/2oz cocoa powder, sifted
100g/4oz apricot jam, melted and cooled slightly
1–2tbsp orange juice
3tbsp rum
275g/10oz good quality plain chocolate (not cooking chocolate)

1. Grease and line a square 17.5cm (7-inch) low-sided baking tin.
2. Place the cake, cocoa powder, jam and walnuts in a mixing bowl. Add the rum and enough orange juice to bind the mixture. Transfer to the tin and smooth the top.
3. Melt the chocolate and pour over the top. Chill overnight in the fridge and cut into 12 squares.

Anyone for tennis?
Get your friends round for tea during Wimbledon fortnight. Serve strawberries and cream, dainty sandwiches, yummy cakes and drink Pimm's. Why not turn any big event into a sporty get-together. Football matches work well – especially the 'big matches' you can't get to like the World Cup. Dress appropriately – paint your face in your team's colours.

Or how about the Olympics, Commonwealth Games, Grand Prix, the Grand National, the Boat Race . . . Don't worry if it's a silly time of day because of the time difference – just match your entertaining to the time. For example, have a 'Big Boy's Breakfast' to end a night watching the match. Don't forget to have some champagne chilling to celebrate or drown your sorrows. Just have fun!

CHAPTER 4
DRINKS PARTIES

A drinks party, or a cheese and wine party with a modern twist (not a giant foil-covered potato 'hedgehog' bristling with cheese, pineapple and cocktail onions in sight!) are great fun and ideal if you want to entertain a large number of guests.

Be realistic about the number of guests you can accommodate at a drinks party. Resist the temptation to 'invite everyone' on the premise that your guests will probably be standing most of the time and so won't need much room. Feeling cosily close is fine, but resembling sardines in a tin is a state your guests won't relish.

A drinks party

Guests love an excuse to dress up for a drinks party – so pay them the compliment of providing an elegant setting – no piles of ironing to walk past, or muddy boots kicking around the hall. Arrangements of seasonal fresh flowers and foliage plants in attractive containers will help create the desired effect without breaking the bank. When you are aiming for elegance, flowers in a single colour appear more stylish than a rainbow of shades.

Drinks parties are most often held in the early evening, but are sometimes held before lunch. They generally last between about two to three hours.

Although food is essential at a drinks party, all you need is a selection of tasty canapés and savouries. A few plates of sweet items like dainty meringues or choux buns that you can produce later are always welcome, but not essential.

Keep your canapés small and neat so they can be eaten in one or two bites. Remember not to overload your plates so that guests can easily select their favourites. Try to have a selection of hot and cold canapés. Making hot canapés is often more time-consuming than putting together an appetising array of cold canapés, so you might like to make the cold ones and buy some good-quality hot canapés to warm at the last minute. (If you serve canapés that have been fried, drain them well on kitchen paper.)

Arrange hot and cold canapés on separate plates – two or three different kinds on each plate. Have a few plates of canapés suitable for vegetarians.

A selection of crudités and dips, bowls of nuts, 'posh' crisps, savoury nibbles and olives around the room for guests to dip into will make the canapés go further.

Speedy cold canapés

- Peel the shells from ready-cooked tiger prawns, leaving the tip of the tail on. Dip each prawn in sweet chilli sauce and then in toasted sesame seeds.
- Thread a basil leaf, a baby mozzarella ball, a wedge of fresh fig and a small roll of prosciutto onto a cocktail stick.
- Peeled hard-boiled quails' eggs speared on a cocktail stick and arranged on a plate with a warm butter dip.
- Two bite-sized pieces of sautéed chicken liver on a cocktail stick.
- Tortilla wedges (see page 57).
- Stilton and walnut bites (see page 58).
- Two bite-sized pieces of sautéed chicken in a spicy marinade on a cocktail stick.
- Shop-bought or home-made blinis with a teaspoon of crème fraîche, a piece of smoked salmon, and a tiny sprig of dill.
- Cut bite-sized circles from brown or white bread, brush with olive oil and pop them into a low oven to crisp. Cool the bread and pipe on a circle of cream cheese. Top with half an olive or a tiny teaspoon of very finely chopped red pepper.
- Cut a panini into thin slices, brush with olive oil and bake in a low oven until crisp. Cool the slices. Spread with a smooth caramelised onion chutney and top with a thin slice of flavoursome cheese and a tiny wedge of green dessert apple.
- Place a tiny teaspoon of hummus onto tortilla chips and sprinkle with a pinch of sweet paprika.
- Remove the stalks from button mushrooms and pipe cream cheese or smooth pâté into the hollows.
- Cut celery into short lengths and pipe soft cheese (you can buy it in tubes) into the hollows.

- Thread cooked king prawns onto sticks with a cube of cucumber and a halved cherry tomato.
- Cut thin 5cm/2 inch strips of cucumber (use a vegetable peeler). Lay a matching strip of smoked salmon on each slice of cucumber and thread onto a cocktail stick in a zigzag fashion.
- Make tiny cheese scones, slit in half and spread each half with either a mixture of blue cheese and butter, or a herb cream cheese. Top with a slice of stuffed olive.
- Wrap thinly sliced ham around a wedge of kiwi fruit and secure with a cocktail stick.

How many canapés?

As a general guide allow:

- 6 to 8 canapés per person for a two-hour party
- 8 to 10 canapés for a four-hour party
- 10 to 12 canapés for a party that lasts all evening

Off the shelf

Save time by buying good-quality hot canapés and bite-sized savouries such as:

- Cocktail-sized Indian starters – pakoras, samosas and bhajis
- Chinese cocktail spring rolls, wontons and prawn toasts
- Cocktail-sized filled savoury tartlets and cones
- Cocktail sushi
- Mini crostini
- Cocktail pizza squares

You can also find cold canapé selections at the supermarket.

Drinks

Serve wine and have a selection of interesting soft drinks on offer for guests who may prefer a nonalcoholic drink, or may be driving. For summer parties fruit punches – with or without alcohol – are popular, while in winter try serving a warming mulled wine or cider.

Have a few glasses of wine poured out ready to offer to your guests as they arrive – unless you are serving champagne. If you are serving a cocktail or a punch have it ready-mixed in a jug or punchbowl. Ask a friend or partner to take on the task of making sure your guests' glasses are replenished during the party. Then you can concentrate on the food.

Watch your budget if you decide to serve spirits, as the cost of the drinks and any mixers you need can soon mount up.

How much drink?

* White wine is generally more popular than red wine, so allow two bottles of white wine to each bottle of red.
* A 750ml (25fl oz) bottle of wine contains five glasses and from a 750ml bottle of champagne expect to get six glasses.
* As a guide allow 2½ glasses of wine for a two-hour drinks party, and one soft drink per person. If you are not serving alcohol allow three glasses per guest.

Winter sangria
(Serves 8)

500ml/18fl oz red wine (Shiraz is ideal)
200ml/7fl oz pure orange juice
220ml/7½fl oz cherry brandy
60ml/2¼fl oz sugar syrup (make by dissolving 40g of caster sugar in 40ml/1½fl oz of boiling water, stirring well, and allowing to cool)
Lemonade
Slices of apple and orange

Pour the sugar syrup, red wine, orange juice and cherry brandy into a large glass jug. Stir and top up with lemonade. Add the slices of fruit.

Mulled cider cup
(Serves 20)

5 small eating apples
4 litres still, dry cider
100g/4oz caster sugar
50g/2oz soft brown sugar
Juice of 6 oranges
Juice of 2 lemons
2tsp freshly ground nutmeg
2tsp ground ginger
15 whole cloves
1 cinnamon stick, broken in half
150ml brandy
6 oranges, sliced

1. Core the apples and, using the point of a knife, score through the skin round the centre of each apple. Place on a plate and microwave for 2 or 3 minutes until just softened (you do not want them to collapse).
2. Put the cider, sugar, orange and lemon juice, and spices into a large pan and heat gently until all the sugar has dissolved, then bring to a serving temperature (do not allow it to boil). Turn off the heat and stir in the brandy. Place the apples and orange slices in the bottom of the punchbowl and pour over the warmed cider cup. Serve in small glasses.

Raspberry and orange cooler
(Serves 20)

100g/4oz frozen raspberries
300ml raspberry juice
1 litre clear apple juice
1 litre blood orange juice
250ml iced water or a couple of large handfuls of ice cubes
Juice of 2 limes
Thin slices of lime and orange
Sprigs of mint

If using fresh raspberries, open freeze them and place into a bag in the freezer (or buy a bag of frozen raspberries). Combine the raspberry juice, apple juice, orange juice, lime juice and water and pour into large glass jugs. Add the frozen raspberries, mint leaves and orange and lime slices.

Anthea's top tips

* Provide plenty of napkins for sticky fingers.
* Spreading plates of canapés around will encourage guests to circulate rather than gather in one place.
* If your party has a Mediterranean theme consider buying some colourful tiles to use as platters.
* If you are really pressed for time why not get a local caterer to supply you with an array of mouthwatering canapés?
* Enlist the help of older children to take round the food and napkins – they love a chance to dress up and feel responsible.

Tortilla wedges

(Makes 20)

1tsp olive oil
1 medium onion, thinly sliced
6 small new potatoes, washed and thinly sliced
2 large red peppers, deseeded, quartered and thinly sliced
2 cloves garlic
6 large eggs
1tsp chilli sauce
2tsp parsley, finely chopped
Seasoning

1. Place the oil into a 20cm (8-inch) lidded nonstick frying pan and spread over the pan. Add the onion and potato slices and cook gently for 15 minutes or until tender. Turn frequently. Add the strips of pepper and garlic and cook for a further 5 minutes.
2. Remove from the heat and spread the vegetables evenly over the base of the pan.
3. Beat the eggs in a bowl, season with salt and pepper, add the chilli sauce and parsley and pour into the pan. Cook the tortilla over a low heat until it is completely set (if you like a brown top on your tortilla place it under the grill for a couple of minutes).
4. Allow the tortilla to cool completely before cutting it into bite-sized wedges.

Stilton and walnut bites
(Makes 20)

150g/6oz Stilton
4 level tsp softened butter
40 walnut halves
Freshly ground black pepper

Crumble the cheese into a small bowl and add the butter. Beat with a fork to combine. Season with black pepper. Sandwich pairs of the walnuts together with the Stilton and butter paste.

* As an alternative you can make the Stilton and butter paste into tiny balls and roll them in finely chopped peanuts.

Herby garlic cheese dip
(Serves about 10)

75ml sour cream
100g/4oz low-fat cream cheese
1 shallot, very finely chopped
1 clove garlic, crushed
2tsp fresh parsley, finely chopped
1tbsp chives, finely snipped
Freshly ground black pepper

Combine all of the ingredients in a bowl, reserving a little of the chives for garnish. Beat together well, transfer into a serving bowl and garnish with the chives. Chill well before serving with a selection of 'vegetable' crisps.

A cheese and wine party with a modern touch

A cheese and wine party can be a relaxing and economical way of entertaining a large group, especially in the winter when barbecues are not practical. They can be held at lunchtime and in the evening.

Another bonus is that once the table is prepared, the hostess can relax and really enjoy the company of her guests.

Give your party a modern twist by hiring the sommelier from a local restaurant or a wine buff from a wine shop to provide your guests with a talk or a tasting. If you've got a friendly specialist cheese shop in your town or a local artisan cheese maker, they might be willing to come along to talk about the mysteries of their craft and give you a tasting session.

The cheeses you choose to serve are a matter of personal preference. You might like to offer a selection of regional English cheeses, or perhaps a collection of Continental cheeses, or even a mix of both. Buy some inexpensive matt black tiles from a DIY store and use a piece of white chalk or white marker to write the names of the cheeses on the tiles, or make attractive labels for the cheeses with information about each of them – where they are made, from which kind of milk, and a description of their flavours.

It's best to have a few large pieces of cheese for people to taste rather than a lot of small pieces. Put each piece of cheese on its own plate or tile so the flavours don't merge. It also means that several guests can serve themselves at the same time. Garnish the plates with watercress, baby salad leaves or herbs. Have a separate knife for each cheese.

You might like to arrange the cheeses on your table in order of 'strength', starting with the mild cheeses and progressing to the strongest ones. Along with popular cheeses try to include some which may be unfamiliar to your guests, so they can indulge in a tasting adventure.

Also serve a selection of fruit – small pears, small apples, grapes, slices of fresh fig – and vegetables such as carrot sticks, red pepper and cucumber batons along with celery sticks and chicory leaves. Leave pears and apples for people to slice themselves.

A selection of chutneys, pickles, relishes, pickled onions or olives can also be added to the food table.

To accompany the cheeses you'll need a selection of fresh bread – include a granary, wholemeal and a French stick. Perhaps you might like to add some speciality breads such as walnut bread, olive bread, onion bread or sun-dried tomato bread. Or you might like to include some of the Continental breads now readily available along with some biscuits and crackers.

To make serving simple for guests, cut butter into small squares or make it into balls or curls. Place the butter in bowls of water with ice cubes to prevent it getting too soft. Have several bowls on the table.

The wines you choose to accompany your cheese are a matter of personal preference. But if you're stuck for inspiration, ask your local wine shop manager for suggestions.

If you decide to serve cheeses all from one country, you might like to choose wines from the same country.

If you serve white wine, chill it for an hour before serving. Red wine should generally be served at room temperature and opened two to three hours before it is poured.

If your cheese and wine party is going on well into the evening, when guests would expect to be having a meal, you may like to end your party by serving a light dessert or coffee and a selection of luxury biscuits and bite-sized dessert cakes.

Calculating quantities
- 150–175g (4–6oz) of cheese per person
- 37–50g (1½–2oz) of butter per person
- 4 pieces of bread per person
- Half a bottle of wine per person

You may need to allow more if the party is held at a time when it replaces a meal.

Here are a few suggestions of wines to complement English cheeses.

Double Gloucester
Bordeaux (French, light red) or Barbaresco (Italian, dry red)

English Cheddar
Barolo (Italian, dry red) or Chateauneuf-du-Pape (French, full-bodied red)

Red Leicester
Valpolicella (Italian, light dry red)

Wensleydale
Anjou Rosé (French, Rosé) or Reisling (German, fruity white)

Lancashire
Alsace (French, fruity dry white) or Fino sherry (dry sherry)

White Stilton
Ruby Port

CHAPTER 5
INFORMAL SUPPERS

After a busy week at work or home, an invitation to an informal Friday evening or weekend supper is a real treat for any guest. No one expects cordon bleu cuisine – good company and a welcoming ambience are as important as the food you serve. A main course that you know you do well, a starter or dessert, and a nice wine are all you need. If time is short it's perfectly acceptable to make use of ready-made accompaniments, a starter, dessert, or even a main course.

But just because you are giving your party an 'informal' tag, don't leave everything to the last minute or let your usual Perfect Housewife standards tumble.

Cheating with style
If you decide to raid the supermarket or deli for ready-made dishes hunt out the premium ranges. The secret is to give the overall impression that the meal is home-made. For example, if you find a main course you want to serve, look on the ingredients list and see if any herbs are used. Then buy some fresh herbs of that kind and use them to garnish the dish. Spend some of the time you will save by not having to cook a main course making home-made vegetable dishes, or a dessert. (If you plan to buy a main course it's a good idea to give it a trial run on the family – you may hate it!)

If you buy a chilled or frozen dessert, avoid any that can't be easily transferred out of their plastic bowls or containers – they're a dead giveaway!

Italian alfresco supper for friends

No one does alfresco dining better than the Italians. We've all seen them on TV – large happy groups sitting at rustic tables under olive trees enjoying freshly cooked food and drinking wine. You may not have the olive trees, but why not try the experience on a warm summer evening?

Keep your dishes simple. For a starter you could serve chunks of ciabatta bread to dip into bowls of flavoured olive oils, and the light-flavoured balsamic vinegars, such as fig, raspberry or sherry balsamic vinegar. Accompany with some of the Continental bottled roasted vegetables in oil from the deli or supermarket such as artichoke hearts, peppers, sun-dried tomatoes, garlic, and also olives. Follow with bowls of your favourite pasta dish with a crisp mixed salad. If you want to serve a sweet course, finish with a fresh fruit salad or an Italian-style dessert. No Italian meal would be complete without wine and, of course, aromatic freshly brewed coffee.

Anthea's top tip

Decorate your table with small containers filled with posies of lavender and herbs – such as lemon balm, rosemary and thyme.

⤜ Alfresco Supper Menu ⤞

Ciabatta chunks with flavoured balsamic vinegar and olive oil dips and a selection of Continental vegetables in oil

———

Your favourite pasta dish served with a large mixed salad

———

Apricot and almond tart with cream or yogurt
Or
Mocha trifle

———

Freshly brewed coffee

Apricot and almond tart
(Serves 8)

250g/9oz mascarpone cheese
200g luxury ready-made fresh custard (with vanilla)
1 bought ready-cooked sweet short crust pastry case
2 large cans apricot halves, drained
40g/1½ oz toasted slivered almonds
2 heaped tbsp apricot jam

1. In a bowl combine the mascarpone cheese and the custard and mix together.
    Spoon into the base of the pastry case and level the top.
2. Take the drained apricots and pat dry on kitchen towel. Arrange in circles on top
    of the custard mixture starting at the outside and moving to the middle. Sprinkle
    over the toasted slivered almonds.
3. Place the jam in a small non-stick saucepan and melt over a low heat. Sieve into a
    small jug and drizzle over the tart. Place in the fridge until needed.

Mocha trifle
(Serves 6)

6 individual frozen chocolate mousses
1 plain chocolate or coffee sponge cake
A miniature of coffee liqueur (Tia Maria or Kahlua)
1 tin pears, drained and chopped
150g/6oz chocolate-covered digestive biscuits, crushed
2tsp instant coffee dissolved in 1tbsp boiling water
1 large carton of luxury custard
300g/½ pint double cream, lightly whipped
50g/2oz grated good-quality dark chocolate

1. Defrost the chocolate mousses. Cut the cake into small squares and place in the
    base of a large glass dessert dish. Drizzle with the liqueur. Add the chopped pears
    to the dish. Spoon the chocolate mousse over and level the top.
2. Sprinkle over the crushed digestive biscuits. Dissolve the instant coffee in boiling
    water and allow to cool. Stir the coffee into the custard and spoon the custard
    over the biscuit layer. Lightly whip the cream and spoon over the custard.
3. Chill for 2 hours. Just before serving decorate with grated dark chocolate.

Chinese New Year supper

You don't have to be a wizard with a wok to create a Chinese New Year feast. It's easy to cheat – and this time it doesn't matter if everyone knows! But if you can knock up a couple of tasty Chinese dishes – and not all Oriental dishes have to be stir-fried at the last minute – your guests will be most impressed. Serve a selection of dishes for everyone to share and a large bowl of fluffy rice. It's usual to set out all the main-course dishes at the same time.

Desserts are not a major feature of Asian cuisine, but you could serve fresh mango slices and lychees to end the meal.

Offer lager or a light wine with the meal and finish with fragrant jasmine or green tea – served without milk or sugar.

Three ways to create a memorable Chinese New Year feast

* Order in a special Chinese New Year feast from your favourite takeaway. Invite each guest to choose one dish from the takeaway menu to build a feast to share.
* Buy in a selection of Chinese starters and meat, fish and vegetable main-course dishes from the supermarket. Add your own boiled rice and some attractive garnishes.
* Cook a couple of simple Chinese dishes and buy other dishes to complete the meal.

Give your decorations an Oriental feel with rich reds and golds, dragons, lanterns and candles. Each year in the Chinese calendar is associated with an animal – incorporate this into your decorations.

You don't need Chinese-style crockery – traditional plates are fine. But if you enjoy Asian food it might be worth investing in a few good-sized rice bowls and matching plates, along with a few Chinese serving dishes and chopsticks. You can pick them up in Chinese stores and some supermarkets.

Experimenting with chopsticks is great fun and leads to much hilarity – but your guests could get quite hungry while they master the art, so give each guest a fork and spoon as well.

The Chinese New Year falls at the end of January or beginning of February in the western calendar. There are 12 years in the Chinese astrological cycle, and each one is associated with an animal.

Rat	1924	1936	1948	1960	1972	1984	1996	2008
Ox	1925	1937	1949	1961	1973	1985	1997	2009
Tiger	1926	1938	1950	1962	1974	1986	1998	2010
Rabbit	1927	1939	1951	1963	1975	1987	1999	2011
Dragon	1928	1940	1952	1964	1976	1988	2000	2012
Snake	1929	1941	1953	1965	1977	1989	2001	2013
Horse	1930	1942	1954	1966	1978	1990	2002	2014
Sheep	1931	1943	1955	1967	1979	1991	2003	2015
Monkey	1932	1944	1956	1968	1980	1992	2004	2016
Rooster	1933	1945	1957	1969	1981	1993	2005	2017
Dog	1934	1946	1958	1970	1982	1994	2006	2018
Pig	1935	1947	1959	1971	1983	1995	2007	2019

In Chinese astronomy it is believed that the animal associated with the year of your birth influences your character. There is an ancient saying that this is 'the animal that hides in your heart'.

How well do you match your animal?

Rat
Hardworking, disciplined, charismatic, charming and sociable. Can be manipulative.

Ox
Dependable, calm, modest, tenacious and logical. Can be stubborn.

Tiger
Rebellious, passionate, generous, impulsive and colourful. Can be impatient.

Rabbit
Sensitive, amiable, cautious, compassionate and artistic. Can be lazy.

Dragon
Self-assured, decisive, ambitious, strong and fiery. Can be eccentric.

Snake
Sensual, graceful, cautious, shrewd and purposeful. Can be possessive.

Horse
Cheerful, popular, intelligent, talkative and open-minded. Can be fickle.

Sheep
Sincere, shy, gentle, compassionate and creative. Can be pessimistic.

Monkey
Quick-witted, inquisitive, competitive, flexible and sociable. Can be jealous.

Rooster
Neat, organised, practical, conservative and responsible. Can be opinionated.

Dog
Honest, intelligent, idealistic, practical and affectionate. Can be judgemental.

Pig
Patient, loyal, hard working, sincere and intelligent. Can be self-indulgent.

Off the shelf

It's so easy to fill up your trolley with a complete Chinese New Year feast. Here's an off-the-shelf menu idea:

A selection of Chinese savouries – prawn toasts, dim sum
Or
Chicken and sweet-corn soup

Sweet and sour pork
Beef and vegetables in black bean sauce
Chicken in lemon sauce
Spicy king prawns
Crispy duck with plum sauce and pancakes
Vegetables in yellow bean sauce
Vegetable spring rolls
Crispy seaweed
Boiled rice

Here are several simple Chinese dishes which are easy to cook from scratch. (If you look at some of the wide range of jars and pouches of Chinese sauces in the supermarket, you'll find recipes on them for more simple dishes you can create in no time at all.)

The secret of preparing Chinese food is to get absolutely everything ready in advance so that all you have to do is add the ingredients to the pan, as they are needed. Remember to slice all of your vegetables into equal-sized pieces so that everything will cook evenly.

Chicken and mango stir-fry
(Serves 4)

1 medium mango, skinned and sliced
3 chicken breasts, skinned and sliced into thin strips
1 bunch of spring onions cut into 5cm/2 inch lengths
1 red pepper, deseeded and sliced into strips
250g bag of ready-to-use stir-fry vegetables
1 clove garlic, crushed
2½cm/1 inch piece of fresh ginger, peeled and grated
3 tbsp soy sauce
1 tbsp sweet chilli sauce
1 level tbsp cornflour dissolved in 3tbsp cold water
4 tbsp vegetable oil

1. Heat 2 tbsp of the oil in a large nonstick frying pan or wok. Cook the chicken for 4–5 minutes, stirring all the time, until it is lightly coloured. Remove from the pan and set aside.
2. Add the remaining oil to the pan and heat. Add the spring onions, pepper, ginger and garlic. Stir-fry for half a minute. Add the mango, the chicken and the bag of prepared stir-fry vegetables and stir together. Add the soy sauce and chilli sauce and cook for 3 minutes until the chicken is completely cooked and the vegetables have slightly softened. Stir in the cornflour and water and cook until the juices have thickened.
3. Serve with boiled rice or noodles.

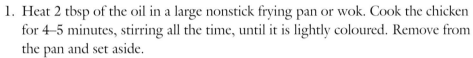

Fish with black bean sauce

(Serves 6)

2 cloves garlic, chopped
150ml/½ pint dry sherry or rice wine
2tbsp black bean sauce
2tbsp soy sauce
1tsp sugar
1tbsp lemon juice
1 level tbsp fresh root ginger, peeled and cut into matchsticks
2tsp vegetable oil
3 large spring onions, thinly sliced
750g/1½lb chunky cod fish fillets, skin removed
To garnish:
Finely shredded lettuce
2 spring onions
½ a red pepper, deseeded and finely sliced

1. Preheat the oven to 180°C/Gas 4.
2. In a small bowl mix together the garlic, dry sherry, black bean sauce, soy sauce, sugar, lemon juice, oil, ginger and chopped spring onions. Lightly oil a lidded ovenproof dish. Lay the fish fillets into the dish and pour over the sauce. Replace the lid. Bake in the oven for 20 minutes or until the fish is cooked through.
3. Arrange a bed of finely shredded lettuce on a serving plate. Remove the fish and place on the lettuce, then spoon over any remaining sauce. Cut the spring onion into fine shreds and sprinkle over the fish. Add the finely sliced red pepper.

Char sui pork
(Serves 8)

900g/2lb pork fillet
2tbsp dark soy sauce
2tbsp hoi sin sauce
2tbsp soft brown sugar
½tsp Chinese five spice powder
¼tsp salt
¼tsp freshly ground black pepper
1tbsp cornflour
1tbsp olive oil
3tbsp runny honey
To garnish:
3 spring onions

1. Trim all of the fat from the pork fillet and place in a shallow ovenproof dish. Combine all of the other ingredients, except the honey, in a small bowl and pour over the pork. Turn the pork several times to coat in the marinade. Chill for several hours or overnight in the fridge.
2. Preheat the oven to 190°C/Gas 5. Take a deep baking tray and place a wire rack in it. Remove the pork from the marinade and place on the wire rack. Roast the pork for 40 minutes or until the juices run clear when you insert a skewer into the centre of the meat. Turn the pork a couple of times during the cooking.
3. Remove the baking tray from the oven and pour the honey over the meat. Return to the oven for 5 minutes. Take the meat from the oven and allow to cool for 10 minutes.
4. Slice the meat into thick 'rounds' and arrange on a serving plate. To garnish, cut the spring onions into short lengths and then into fine strips. Sprinkle over the pork.

Garnishes

Dishes at Chinese feasts are always beautifully garnished. Try some of these vegetable garnishes:

- Peel the skin from tomatoes in one continuous circular strip from the top to the bottom. Wrap the skin round your finger to form a rose.
- Make spring onion tassels. Cut spring onions into 7.5cm (3-inch) lengths. Taking a sharp knife, cut through half the length of the spring onion several times to create a 'witch's broom' effect. Place the cut spring onion in cold water and leave for an hour. The cut ends will curl to form tassels.
- Take a peeled carrot and cut a small v-shape down the whole length. Cut narrow rings of carrot – they will be heart-shaped.
- Cut 2.5cm (1-inch) lengths from a cucumber. As though you were slicing the cucumber into rings, cut three-quarters of the way through the piece so that each ring is still attached at the base. Fold every second slice in half so that it is held down by the slices on either side.
- Take a radish and make vertical slits (resembling petals) around the radish from the base to the top. Place the radish in cold water and the 'petals' will open to form a radish flower.

A 'desserts' party

Try something a little different – throw a dessert party. For those with a sweet tooth the prospect is sheer bliss. And for the hostess there is no need to worry about balancing starters and main courses.

Aim to serve a selection of different kinds of desserts for your guests to try – from gooey chocolate extravaganzas to all-time favourites like sticky toffee pudding, apple pie and exotic fruit salads. Many desserts can be frozen ahead, or cooked in advance, so it's a good idea to include some of these. Then on the day all you'll need to do is make any last-minute desserts, prepare the drinks and set the scene for your party.

To work out how many desserts to prepare, and how many portions you need, expect guests to want to try about three or four different desserts in the course of an evening.

Serve a dessert wine and a nonalcoholic exotic fruit punch. End the meal with coffee and some hand-made chocolates.

Banana and ginger delight
(Serves 6)

4 thick slices of ginger cake
3tbsp rum
4 bananas
2tbsp lemon juice
300ml/½ pint fromage frais or whipping cream
4tbsp soft light-brown sugar

1. Cut the cake into squares and arrange in the base of a low-sided heat-proof dish. Drizzle with the rum.
2. Slice the bananas and toss in the lemon juice to prevent them turning brown. Arrange over the cake. Top with the fromage frais or whipped cream. Sprinkle the brown sugar over the top.
3. Place under a preheated grill for 2–3 minutes until the sugar has melted. Chill for several hours before serving.

Orange and rum butter pancakes
(Serves 6)

12 thin pancakes (home-made or bought)
175g/6oz butter
175g/6oz soft brown sugar
3tbsp rum
4 oranges, cut into wedges

1. Make the pancakes and place on a plate, cover with foil and keep warm in a low oven. If you buy pancakes, cover with foil and warm.
2. Make the rum butter by beating together the butter, sugar and rum. (The rum butter can be made in advance and chilled or frozen.)
3. Place a knob of rum butter in the centre of each hot pancake, fold in half, then in half again to form a triangle. Arrange on a serving plate and sprinkle with icing sugar. Serve with orange wedges.

Tangy citrus ice cream gateau
(Serves 6)

1 slab of ready-made Madeira cake
500ml tub crème fraiche
1 jar good-quality lemon curd
8 ready-made meringues
1 lemon
2 tbsp caster sugar
100ml water

1. Cut a circle of baking parchment to fit the base of a 20cm/8inch round spring form cake tin.
2. Cut the Madeira cake into slices and use to line the base of the cake tin. Fill in any gaps between the slices of cake with small slivers of cake.
3. Break the meringues into chunky pieces into a bowl. Add the crème fraiche and gently fold together, trying not to crush the meringue pieces. Tip the lemon curd into a bowl and stir with a spoon.
4. Place large tablespoons of the crème fraiche mixture and smaller tablespoons of the lemon curd onto the cake base. When you have used all of the mixtures level the surface, but do not stir. Lift the cake tin and tap lightly on the work surface to ensure that the mixture is well packed down.
5. Cover with clingfilm and freeze for up to two weeks.

To serve the ice cream gateaux:
1. Make a lemon sugar syrup by finely paring the skin from the lemon and cutting into thin matchsticks. (Avoid the white pith as this is bitter.) Place in a saucepan with the water and caster sugar. Bring to the boil stirring all the time and then simmer gently until you have a light syrup. Allow to cool completely.
2. Take the cake out of the freezer 20 minutes before serving and place on a serving plate. Drizzle over the lemon syrup and lemon strands and place the gateau in the fridge so that it softens slightly.

Champagne strawberries
(Serves 4 to 6)

A large punnet of fresh strawberries, hulled and washed
Champagne or sparkling white wine
A few mint leaves
Dessert biscuits

Fill champagne or wine glasses with strawberries. Chill in the fridge for about an hour. Just before serving pour champagne over the strawberries and decorate with a pair of mint leaves. Serve immediately with crisp dessert biscuits.

Boys' cook-in
Turn the tables on the boys and consign them to the kitchen. You and your girlfriends go off to the pub for a few relaxing drinks while the boys cook supper.
Set them to make proper dishes (not something from the local takeaway), lay the table and do the washing up!
You might even be able to persuade them to dress as chefs and waiters for the evening!

I once had a poster in my larder saying, 'Life is too short – eat pudding first' – and I'm sure many would agree. Share the work by asking each of your guests to bring a dessert. Be ready to offer some suggestions like, 'It would be nice to have a cheesecake' or 'A tart would be wonderful', so you don't end up with six trifles. Try serving dessert champagne – it's gorgeous.

CHAPTER 6
DINNER PARTIES

If giving a dinner party fills you with dread – don't panic. The days of hostesses struggling to stay calm while juggling seven-course eating extravaganzas at home are long gone. All you need for a successful dinner party are three simple courses, a small group of compatible guests, a relaxed and stylish atmosphere . . . and a happy hostess.

Most guests will take the opportunity to dress up when they are invited to dinner so return the compliment by making the event 'special'. Pay attention to your table setting and to lighting. You want subdued lighting for dining but not so dim that guests wish they had brought a torch. Make time to clean and tidy any rooms your guests may glimpse – your hall, dining room, lounge and bathroom should sparkle like a new pin.

Remember not to invite more guests than your table can accommodate comfortably – no one wants to sit shoulder to shoulder for several hours, however friendly they are! Get your invitations out in good time.

The dishes you choose should reflect not only the occasion and your guests, but also the season, the time you have available and your budget. Think about colour, flavours, texture and variety when you are deciding on your menu. Plan the main course first and then a starter and dessert to complement it. Try to balance a rich main-course dish by serving a plain starter and a refreshing dessert.

Choose recipes you are confident with, unless there's time for a trial run. If you are short of time serve a cold starter and a prepare-ahead dessert, then you can concentrate on the main course and its accompaniments. Or make a hot starter and a main course that can be prepared in advance, then reheated and served. Classic dishes such as coq au vin or a rich beef casserole are perfect fare for winter dinner parties. In the summer look for lighter dishes such as an all-in-one baked chicken dish including summer vegetables. Unless you are a really accomplished cook, dishes that have to be pan-fried or grilled while your guests wait between courses, like steaks or salmon, are best avoided.

Most people can't resist desserts so opt for something delicious and perhaps a little decadent (but have a selection of fresh fruit available as well). Finish your meal by offering a cheeseboard, or moving straight on to freshly brewed coffee and a few hand-made chocolates.

Off the shelf

If you are short of time check out the delicatessen and supermarket for simple time-savers.

For starters you could try:

* A pâté or mousse served with crisp Melba toasts.
* Roasted vegetables served on a bed of salad leaves with feta cheese cubes.
* Thinly sliced prosciutto wrapped around a piece of mozzarella and a peach quarter or a slice of fresh fig.

Also look out for:

* Interesting frozen or chilled potato dishes. (Remember to discard the horrid plastic trays and transfer to your own dishes before cooking, as it is easier to do when they are cold.)
* Ready-prepared vegetables that you can just cook and serve.
* Luxury desserts that you can give a home-made look by adding your own decoration. For example, pipe rosettes of cream onto a dark chocolate torte and top with chocolate coffee beans and mint leaves. Or boil some thinly pared orange rind in a light sugar syrup, drain on kitchen paper, allow to get cold and place in the centre of a classic French lemon torte.
* For a delicious 'fire and ice' dessert buy a bag of mixed red-berry fruits, and warm gently in a saucepan with a little sugar, if necessary, and a splash of rum or brandy. Serve spooned over luxury vanilla ice cream with crisp dessert biscuits.

Anthea's top tip

A delicious alternative to serving chocolates with coffee is to offer individual ice-cream desserts nestling in a bowl of ice.

⤐ A menu for winter ⤏

Baked Camembert with redcurrant sauce

Coq au vin
Mashed potatoes
Green beans, broccoli and baby carrots

Citrus brandy creams

Coffee and chocolates

❧ A menu for summer ❧

Smoked salmon with wholemeal bread and lemon wedges

Summer baked chicken with fennel
Green beans and asparagus
Mixed baby-leaf salad
Baked baby new potatoes in their jackets

Jamaican pineapple

Cheeseboard
Coffee and iced dessert chocolates

Baked Camembert with redcurrant sauce
(Serves 6)
These need to made just before you are ready to serve them.

6 individual Camembert portions, packaging removed
4 tbsp redcurrant jelly
1 tbsp white vinegar
Baby mixed salad leaves

1. Preheat the oven to 170°C/Gas 3.
2. Arrange a small handful of baby salad leaves on six small plates.
3. Put the redcurrant jelly and the vinegar in a small nonstick saucepan and heat gently until the jelly has melted. Keep warm.
4. Place the cheese portions on a nonstick baking tray and heat in the oven for 8–10 minutes until they are warm and soft. You do not want them to collapse. Immediately place on the plates by the side of the salad leaves and drizzle the warmed redcurrant jelly over the cheese. Serve with Melba toast.

Coq au vin

(Serves 6 to 8)

Traditionally coq au vin would be marinated in a reduced wine stock for 24 hours but here is a simplified version which is perfect for dinner parties.

1 x 2.25kg/5lb chicken, cut into joints
175g/6oz streaky bacon, cubed
20 baby onions, skinned and left whole
225g/8oz button mushrooms, wiped
A bouquet garni (made from 6 parsley stalks, 4 sprigs of thyme and 2 bay leaves tied into a bundle with string)
2 garlic cloves
725ml/1¼ pints full-bodied red wine
3 medium carrots, cut into thick circles
2 celery stalks, cut into 2cm/¾ inch pieces
1 tbsp butter
1 tbsp vegetable oil
Salt and freshly ground black pepper

To thicken:
1 tbsp butter
1 tbsp flour

To garnish:
2 tbsp fresh parsley, roughly chopped

1. Ask your butcher to cut the chicken into portions for you and also to cut you 175g/6oz of unsmoked back bacon in three slices so that it can be cubed.
2. To make thickening, combine the butter and the flour in a small bowl and mix with a fork until it forms a paste. Cover with cling film and put in the fridge until it is needed to thicken the cooking liquid.
3. Melt the butter and oil in a large frying pan and fry the chicken joints – a few at a time – until they are golden. Remove from the pan with a slotted spoon and place in a large saucepan or flameproof casserole dish – it needs to be large enough to allow the chicken joints to be arranged in a single layer. Fry the bacon, onions, garlic cloves, carrots and celery for five minutes. Transfer to the pan with the chicken. Add the bouquet garni and the red wine. Season with pepper and a little salt (you can add more later if needed).

4. Bring the pan to the boil and simmer with a lid on for 50–60 minutes or until the chicken is tender. Add the mushrooms for the last 15 minutes of cooking time.
5. At the end of the cooking time remove and discard the bouquet garni. Using a slotted spoon transfer the chicken and vegetables to a large serving dish and place in a low oven to keep warm.
6. Bring the liquid remaining in the pan to the boil and boil until it has reduced by about a third. Then gradually add small pieces of the flour/butter paste to the liquid, stirring all the time, until you reach the required thickness. Pour the liquid over the chicken and vegetables. Just before serving garnish with fresh chopped parsley.

Citrus brandy creams

(Serves 6)

This is a simple and refreshing dessert that can be prepared a few hours in advance and kept in the fridge.

2 medium oranges, juice and zest, grated
150g/6oz caster sugar
4tbsp brandy
900ml/1½ pint double cream
To decorate:
A little orange zest
4 fresh mint leaves

1. Place the orange zest, orange juice, brandy and sugar in a small bowl, cover with clingfilm and leave for a few hours until the sugar has completely dissolved. Remove a little of the zest for decoration and place on a pad of kitchen paper to drain.
2. Frost the rim of six wine glasses by dipping the rim into a saucer containing egg white, then in a saucer containing granulated sugar. Set aside to dry.
3. When you are ready to make the dessert, whip the cream until it forms soft peaks. Continue whisking while gradually adding the orange, sugar and brandy mixture in a steady stream. Whisk gently until the cream is the texture of mousse. Spoon into the wine glasses and decorate with the reserved zest and a couple of mint leaves. Refrigerate for at least 4 hours.

Summer baked chicken with fennel
(Serves 6)

6 boneless chicken breasts
1tbsp olive oil
3–4 cloves garlic, thinly sliced
1 red pepper, deseeded and sliced
1 green pepper, deseeded and sliced
2 bulbs of fennel, trimmed and thinly sliced
12 cherry tomatoes
1 large can chopped tomatoes
1 small can chopped tomatoes
2tsp sugar
75ml/3fl oz white wine
150ml/5fl oz chicken stock
1tbsp balsamic vinegar
Salt and freshly ground black pepper
8 black olives
Handful of whole basil leaves

1. Heat the oil in a nonstick frying pan and cook the chicken until golden on both sides. Transfer to a large low-sided ovenproof dish.
2. Add the pepper, garlic and fennel to the frying pan and fry for 5 minutes. Add the chopped tomatoes, cherry tomatoes, sugar, white wine, stock and balsamic vinegar and bring to the boil. Season to taste. Pour over the chicken and bake for 30 to 40 minutes or until the chicken is cooked through.
3. Scatter over the black olives if using and the whole basil leaves.

Jamaican pineapple
(Serves 6)

2 small ripe pineapples
50g/2oz butter
6tbsp muscovado sugar
8tbsp dark rum
6tbsp water
Mint leaves to garnish

1. Remove the skin, leaves and the sharp 'eyes' from the pineapples. Cut them into quarters vertically. Remove the hard core from the centre and slice each pineapple wedge into 6 circles.
2. Gently sauté the pineapple in the butter until it is lightly coloured (don't let the butter burn or it will be inedible). Remove the pineapple from the pan and place in a bowl. Sprinkle the sugar into the pan, add the water and heat until the sugar has melted and you have a light syrup. Add the dark rum. Pour over the pineapple. Refrigerate until ready to use.
3. Serve hot or cold. When you are ready to serve remove the pineapple from the syrup using a slotted spoon and arrange on six small plates. Pour over the rum syrup and decorate with mint leaves. Serve with a scoop of good-quality vanilla ice cream and a crisp dessert biscuit.

Setting the scene
Treat your table as a canvas on which to create your masterpiece. Make it simple and stylish.
- Start with crisp table linen. White is the traditional favourite, and sets off any decorations beautifully.
- Keep candles, if you use them, below the eye-line of your guests and keep flowers low and simple. Three tiny glass or silver vases bearing a single flower of the same colour, or tiny sprigs of lavender and rosemary, look delightful.
- Always use cloth napkins. Think of novel ways to present the napkins.

Setting the table

Whether the meal is relaxed or more formal, setting the table follows a simple pattern:

- Arrange your cutlery on the table in the order it will be used – working from the outside, in towards the plate.
- The blades of knives should always face inwards. If you are serving soup, the soup spoon goes outside the knives.
- Forks go on the left and knives on the right.
- A dessert spoon and fork can be placed across the top of the setting with the bowl of the spoon facing to the left and the prongs of the fork facing right. The dessert spoon should be placed above the fork.
- Knives or forks not used by the guests are removed when the main course is cleared and the dessert cutlery is moved to the sides of the place setting before dessert is served.
- A side plate is placed by the forks and a butter knife across the plate with the end of its handle facing the edge of the table.
- Glasses – one for water, a small wine glass for white wine and a larger glass for red wine – are placed above the point of the main knife.
- Place napkins in the centre of the place setting, on the side plate or in one of the glasses.
- Condiments (salt, pepper, mustard, etc.) are placed near to the centre of the table if there are six to eight people sitting down to dinner. For a larger dinner party it's usual to have two identical sets at either end of the table.

Napkin ring ideas

- Make a napkin ring with a piece of narrow velvet or satin ribbon and tuck a sprig of lavender or rosemary under it.
- Head for your local fabric shop and rummage through the remnant box for unusual trimmings like lace, pearls, ribbon flowers or tiny tassels to make napkin rings.

DINNER PARTY TIPS

- Keep the numbers small. If it's your first attempt at hosting a dinner party invite close friends – they'll build your confidence, and you'll be raring to go next time.
- Chill champagne for as long as possible. The lower the temperature the lower the pressure in the bottle – so the cork won't fly out.
- Invest in a good-quality waterproof protective covering for your table, and then you won't have to worry about damage from spilled drinks or hot dishes.
- If you are using mats instead of a tablecloth make sure they are heatproof and that you have enough on the centre of the table to receive hot dishes.
- If your tablecloth is too small, cover the table with a white sheet and lay a pretty small white tablecloth over it.
- Water should be served from a jug and wine from the bottle.
- Use a jug with a pinched spout to prevent ice and large pieces of fruit splashing into the glass – or onto a guest.
- If you forget to warm the plates, put them in a sink of very hot water. Leave for five minutes, then dry. Or pop them in the microwave for a minute or two with a glass of water.
- Give your glasses a sparkle by donning rubber gloves and rinsing them in a bowl of really hot water. Allow to air-dry right-side up. When they are completely dry polish with a lint-free cloth.
- Prepare your coffee tray and after-dinner chocolates in advance.

Anthea's top tip

If conversation is moving nicely and you don't want to interrupt the flow, serve coffee at the table. But if it's grinding to a halt with long awkward silences, moving the guests to another room for coffee will often reignite the conversational sparkle.

A romantic Valentine's Day dinner

The setting, the ambience and the mood you create are as important as the food you serve to your loved one. Aim for elegance – you don't want it to look too contrived.

Candlelight and sweet music may be an old cliché but it's still the essence of romance. Choose music to reflect the mood, or to evoke special memories – but keep the volume down. Dinner by candlelight is magical – but make sure you can still gaze into each other's eyes . . . and see what you're eating. Remember to snuff out the candles at the end of the meal.

Opt for a simple menu and choose food you both enjoy. Try to choose a main course that won't require you to disappear into the kitchen for more than a few minutes – you don't want to break the spell! Dishes that can be prepared in advance, half-prepared and finished at the last minute, or will cook happily in the oven while you are getting ready, are perfect.

Make your table look elegant. It's the perfect excuse to use your best white table linen and fine china. Keep your table decorations simple but chic.

Remember to give the house a good clean and tidy – it'll do nothing for romance if you have to step over discarded toys and piles of magazines to reach your beautifully decorated table.

❧ A romantic dinner for two ❧

Grilled peppers, Parma ham and mozzarella

⸺ ◆ ⸺

Glazed honey and mustard chicken
Broccoli and asparagus
Potato gratin

⸺ ◆ ⸺

Chocolate fondant pudding
Coffee and hand-made chocolates

Glazed honey and mustard chicken
(Serves 2)

1tbsp wholegrain mustard
Juice of half a lemon
2 tbsp runny honey
2 chicken breasts
2tsp olive oil
Half a lemon, cut into 4 wedges
4 cherry tomatoes
1 small red onion, cut into 6 wedges

1. Preheat the oven to 190°C/Gas 5. Combine the mustard, lemon juice and honey in a small bowl.
2. Place a teaspoon of the oil into an ovenproof baking dish and spread around the base. Add the chicken breasts to the dish and spoon over the mustard, lemon and honey mixture.
3. Place the second teaspoon of the oil into a bowl and add the cherry tomatoes, onion wedges and lemon wedges. Toss to coat with the oil and place the vegetables around the chicken in the dish.
4. Bake for 25 to 30 minutes or until the chicken is cooked through. Remove the chicken breasts from the dish and cut into 4 pieces diagonally. Transfer the vegetables onto a serving plate and top with the chicken.

Chocolate fondant pudding
(Serves 2)

A little butter to grease dishes
Cocoa for dusting
100g/4oz dark chocolate (at least 70% cocoa solids), chopped
1 egg, plus 1 extra yolk
50g/2oz caster sugar
60g/2½oz butter
25g/1oz plain flour
Raspberries and mint leaves to serve

Anthea's top tip

Arrange with the grandparents or a friend to let the children sleep over. With the little ones out of the way, your partner might even treat you to breakfast in bed the next morning! Don't forget to put the phone on answerphone.

1. Preheat the oven to 180C/Gas 4 and lightly grease 2 medium-sized ramekins with butter. Dust the base and sides with cocoa.
2. Place the chocolate in a bowl and suspend over a saucepan of barely simmering water – make sure the bowl does not touch the surface of the hot water. Allow the chocolate to melt and then stir with a dry spoon. Remove the bowl from the heat to allow the chocolate to cool slightly while you continue to make the puddings.
3. Using an electric whisk, whisk the caster sugar, butter and eggs together in a bowl until the mixture is pale and fluffy and has thickened. Fold the melted chocolate into the mixture, followed by the flour and divide equally between the two ramekins. Place in the oven and bake for 15 to 16 minutes until the tops are risen and set.
4. Place each of the ramekins on individual plates alongside a handful of raspberries decorated with a pair of mint leaves.
5. Serve the pudding accompanied by a small jug of double cream.

Burns Night dinner

We all need something to celebrate in dark, dreary January, so why not join the Scots and throw a Burns Night dinner for your friends. It's something different and a great excuse for a party that'll soon put your guests in the mood for a Highland fling. You may not want to follow the time-honoured format of the event but just choose a few of the traditional elements and have fun.

Traditionally at a Burns Night supper haggis is served with 'champit tatties and bashed neeps' – mashed potatoes and swede. This is followed by crannachan – a raspberry, toasted pinhead oatmeal and cream dessert – and a tassie o' coffee.

If your guests are unfamiliar with haggis it's a good idea to serve it as a starter, so they can just have a taste. You could opt to serve a 'vegetarian' haggis, which tastes delicious. (You can find haggis and vegetarian haggis in some supermarkets or have one mail-ordered from Scotland. You might also be able to get miniature cocktail haggis, the size of quails' eggs.) And don't worry about the mysteries of cooking a haggis, it's already cooked when you buy it so all you have to do is reheat and serve.

Anthea's top tip

Ask any Scottish guests to wear the kilt and invite other guests to get into the mood by adding a piece of tartan to their party gear – a bow tie, a tie, a waistcoat, a scarf or wrap, or a tartan ribbon in their hair.

Follow the haggis starter with your favourite rich beef or venison casserole (made well in advance and frozen) and end the meal with crannachan, coffee and mini rounds of shortbread.

Set the scene by covering your table with a crisp white linen tablecloth. Tie narrow tartan ribbons round your napkins and tuck a sprig of heather underneath – or a miniature of malt whisky or whisky liqueur.

Burns Night and the haggis – the history

The haggis gained its literary fame when Robert Burns penned his famous 'Address to the Haggis' in the eighteenth century. Its ceremonial eating began soon after the poet's death in 1796 when friends gathered on his birthday to take 'supper' – as the Scot's call this traditional meal – in his memory.

The basic format for the evening has remained almost unchanged around the world since that first occasion and begins with a few words of welcome from the host and the reciting of the Selkirk Grace.

> Some hae meat and canna eat
> And some wad eat that want it;
> But we hae meat and we can eat,
> And sae the Lord be thankit.

A piper then leads the chef who ceremoniously carries the haggis to the table – if you haven't got a handy piper among your friends perhaps you could find a recording of some bagpipe music and play a short snatch. The 'Address to the Haggis' is then read by a guest and when he reaches the line 'an cut you up wi' ready slight' he cuts open the haggis with a knife. After the reading of the address, guests all rise and toast the haggis in malt whisky – usually the first of many drams! During the meal a toast is also drunk to 'the lassies'.

For the full version of the 'Address to the Haggis', and to hear it being read aloud, visit:
www.visitscotland.com/aboutscotland/explorebymap/features/burnsaddress2

Ideas for haggis starters

Heat the haggis according to the instructions on the packaging and then try any of these:

- Remove the skin from two cocktail haggises, thread on small wooden skewers and keep warm. To serve drizzle with melted rowan jelly or redcurrant jelly Accompany with a garnish of baby salad leaves.
- Take a shop-bought or home-made pastry tartlet case and place a small amount of haggis in the bottom. Top with a teaspoon of mashed potato and a teaspoon of mashed swede, then add plenty of freshly ground black pepper. Serve warm.
- Bake baby new potatoes in their skins. Cut in half, scoop out the potato and fill the empty shells with a small amount of hot haggis. Top with a few finely sliced spring onions fried in a little butter. Garnish with parsley or salad leaves.
- Place a tablespoon of haggis on baked slices of baguette (brush both sides of the bread with olive oil and bake in a low oven until crisp and golden). Keep warm and just before serving drizzle with rowan or redcurrant jelly. Allow two circles of bread per person.

* If you have any haggis left over, and discover you love the stuff, it makes a great lunch as a filling for a baked potato accompanied by a large salad. Or make a chicken Balmoral (the Scottish relative of a Kiev!). Make a slit in the side of a chicken breast, stuff it with haggis and bake in a foil parcel in a moderate oven (180C/Gas 4) until the chicken is cooked through. Serve for supper with green beans and minted new potatoes.

Crannachan
(Serves 8)

125g/4½oz medium (pinhead) oatmeal, toasted
600ml/20fl oz double cream
4tsp runny heather honey
5tbsp whisky
500g/1lb fresh raspberries
For decoration:
A few raspberries

1. Toast the oatmeal in a dry frying pan until it is golden (keep the pan moving so it does not burn and become bitter). Remove from the heat and allow to get completely cold.
2. Lightly whip the cream and fold in the oatmeal. Fold in the whisky and honey.
3. Place a layer of the cream mixture into 8 wine glasses, followed by a layer of raspberries. Top with another layer of cream. Decorate each dessert with a few raspberries.

CHAPTER 7
BUFFETS

Buffets are a versatile and practical way of serving food at a party when you have more than eight to ten guests to entertain. But they can still be impressive, whether you are serving a finger buffet at a drinks party, a fork buffet for a relaxed evening with friends, or a full-scale buffet banquet for grand occasions such as weddings and anniversaries. Buffets can be served at any time of the day.

The bonus of a buffet, especially for a lone hostess, is that, once the food is laid out, guests can help themselves leaving her to simply watch over the buffet table, replenish dishes if necessary, and circulate.

The buffet table takes centre stage so spend time deciding on your decorations – aim for something stylish, sophisticated and uncluttered. A floral centrepiece or arrangement of fruit and foliage provides an attractive focal point.

Make your preparations well in advance, whether you are planning a small or a large party, and get as much done as you can before the day.

Buffet basics

Decide:

- How many guests to invite – think about the space you have. If it's a summer party you may be able to use the garden, weather permitting – but don't bank on it!
- Whether you want to serve a finger buffet, a simple fork buffet or a full buffet with three courses.
- Your budget for food and drinks – it's easy for costs to spiral out of control especially when catering for large numbers.
- The dishes and the drinks you plan to use. Make lists of everything you will need to buy.
- How to decorate your home and buffet table. Will there be a theme?
- If you need to hire china, cutlery or glassware. (If you are planning an event over Christmas and the New Year make sure that you order anything you need early, as companies can be very busy at this time of the year.)

A finger buffet

A finger buffet is ideal for parties that are planned to last for only a couple of hours such as a drinks party. A mouthwatering selection of hot and cold canapé-style bites, such as tiny savoury tartlets, are all that is needed. A few plates of sweet bites such as mini cream-filled meringues and small éclairs are always appreciated, but not essential. Serve white and red wine and a selection of soft drinks. Or you may like to serve a punch or wine cup.

You can hand the food round on plates or arrange it on several small tables. Serving finger food on tables allows guests to help themselves and frees the hostess to circulate among the guests.

Fork buffet

A fork buffet is incredibly versatile and an ideal choice for entertaining larger groups at home. Once you've created a beautiful buffet table, filled with simple but irresistible dishes, you can relax and wait to be showered with compliments.

The food

A fork buffet should be exactly that – food that your guests can easily eat with a fork, perched at a table or on their laps. So choose your dishes carefully – there's nothing worse than trying to fight with food, while trying to balance a glass and carry out an intelligent conversation at the same time. Avoid dishes with lashings of sauce that could dribble off the plates onto your guests' knees, or large pieces of meat, which if attacked with a fork are almost guaranteed to whiz across the room like flying saucers!

If you are entertaining a group of less than twenty – any more and most homes would feel overcrowded – then two, or at most three main dishes are sufficient.

A choice of a hot and a cold dish or just cold dishes are usually included on a buffet table, along with accompaniments – rice, pasta or potatoes – and appropriate vegetables or salads. If you have vegetarian or vegan guests serve at least one suitable main course.

Anthea's top tip

My favourite buffet dessert is so simple – a bowl of meringues (home-made or shop-bought ones that look authentic and not like blocks of chalk), a bowl of strawberries and a bowl of whipped cream.

Choose desserts that can be made in advance or frozen ahead and decorated on the day. Cold desserts are ideal and a choice of two is plenty. Avoid giant bowls of mousse or trifles, as these can quickly look messy. Individual desserts, bowls of fruit salad, or cheesecakes and tarts that can be cut into slices, are simpler.

> A cheeseboard accompanied by a selection of biscuits and fruit – grapes, slices of fresh fig and kiwi slices – followed by freshly brewed coffee and perhaps some hand-made chocolates – makes the perfect finale.

Drinks

Serve red and white wine, and a refreshing fruit- or wine-based punch. Remember to have a selection of soft drinks available.

Chill white wine in the fridge for two hours before serving. Or if you haven't space, put the bottles in large plastic buckets with ice for an hour.

Most red wines are served at room temperature, though some may be chilled. Check on the label or ask your wine merchant.

Which wines you serve is a matter of personal choice. However many people prefer sweeter wines with the dessert course and a fresh, crisp white wine with the main course.

Arranging a buffet table

Position the buffet table so it can be easily accessed with no bottlenecks. It's a good idea to pull it away from the wall so guests can move around three sides and you can reach the back to easily replace and remove dishes. Place the centrepiece towards the back of the table. Make sure that it is stable and not too high. Arrange food on the table in a logical way with complementary dishes near each other, so that guests don't have to stretch across or double back. A simple way is to start at the back corner of one side, work down that side, along the front and up the second side.

For example:

1. The plates
2. Hot dishes
3. Accompaniments to hot dishes
4. Cold dishes
5. Salads
6. Pickles, sauces and relishes
7. Breadbasket
8. Forks and knives
9. Napkins

Remove all of the first-course dishes when the guests have finished and clear any debris from the table. Lay out the desserts and biscuits and cheese along with plates, cutlery and more napkins.

BUFFET TIPS

- Position the food tables away from radiators.
- Make sure that your table is covered with a waterproof protective cloth under the tablecloth. Spills are unavoidable.
- If you do not have a large enough table, arrange food on smaller tables. You could have cold dishes and their accompaniments on one table, and hot dishes and their accompaniments on another.
- Avoid congestion around the buffet table by serving drinks from a separate table.
- Arrange chairs in groups around the room, and if possible have a couple of conveniently placed tables where elderly guests and children will feel more comfortable.
- Allow a pause between courses to give guests time to relax and savour their food.
- Serve salad dressing separately so that delicate salad vegetables don't wilt.
- Always decant pickles and chutneys into bowls. A plate under each of the bowls will catch any drips and give guests somewhere to lay the serving spoon.
- No nasty plastic butter tubs on the table!
- Make sure you have serving spoons, tongs, etc. by each dish.
- If you don't feel confident roasting a turkey or gammon, or cooking a large side or whole salmon, find a reputable caterer to do it for you.

Buffet suggestions

Simple hot dishes:

- Baked chicken dishes
- Curries
- Rich casseroles
- Baked pasta dishes
- Mince dishes – chilli con carne, lasagne and moussaka
- Seafood gratins
- Paellas
- Spicy tagines

Simple cold dishes:

- Game pies
- Savoury tarts
- Cold roast turkey (sliced very thinly)
- Cold boiled or baked ham (sliced very thinly)
- A side of salmon or whole salmon

Estimating quantities

As a rough guide for each person allow:

Starters:

Soup	250ml/8fl oz
Prawns and shellfish	75g/3oz
Fish	100g/4oz

Main courses and accompaniments:

Fish	175g/6oz
Meat	175–225g/6–8oz
Chicken, duck, turkey	175–225g/6–8oz
Vegetables	150g/6oz
Baked potatoes	1 potato (150–200g/6–8oz)
Roast potatoes	2–3 pieces
Boiled new potatoes	3–5 potatoes
Rice (uncooked)	50g/2oz
Pasta (uncooked)	75–100g/3–4oz
Bread	1 roll or equivalent
Salad leaves	50g/2oz

A Buffet Banquet

This is entertaining on a grand scale – and usually reserved for very special occasions, such as weddings and special anniversaries. It is a major undertaking, and not something to be embarked on without a good deal of help from friends or at least some reliable and experienced hired help. But to be honest, unless numbers are reasonably small, most people are happier to leave food preparation and service on this scale to professional caterers.

Generally, because of the numbers involved, buffet banquets are held at hired venues or in a marquee. The fact that you will probably be entertaining away from your familiar surroundings is another good reason to hand it over to the experts.

Aim to balance the formality of a smart dinner party with the simplicity of a buffet. The setting is crucial. Create an elegant ambience with beautifully decorated surroundings and tables.

At formal buffets guests are seated at either large tables or a number of smaller tables. The place settings at the table are laid in the usual way for formal entertaining.

Plan your menu carefully and keep a tight rein on the budget. Three or four courses is all you need when entertaining on this scale. It's a good idea to choose a cold starter and dessert. The starter can be placed on the tables shortly before the guests sit down; they then serve themselves to the main course from the buffet. The dessert is either brought to the tables or served from the buffet. Wine can be placed on the tables or served by waiting staff. If coffee is served it is often most convenient if it is brought to the tables.

Even if you are preparing the food for the buffet yourself you will need to hire some help on the day – to move the food from your home, prepare the tables, lay out the buffet, see to the drinks, assist guests while the main course is being served, remove used china, and serve any courses to the table. There will also be all the clearing away and washing up to be taken care of!

Secrets of success

* Assign yourself only the tasks that you can realistically manage on the day – you won't be the Perfect Hostess if you are hassled and you certainly won't enjoy the big day.
* At a formal buffet have a seating plan on a board near the entrance to the dining room so that guests can find their places easily.
* If you do hire caterers, you will still need to 'project manage' the arrangements at every stage to ensure that you are not disappointed on the day.

Planning the menu for a buffet banquet

* Decide whether you are going to serve a hot buffet, a cold buffet, or a combination of hot and cold dishes.
* Select dishes that complement one another.
* Balance rich main courses by serving simple salad starters and light desserts.
* Choose hot dishes that will not spoil if they have to be kept hot.
* Make the starter light and attractive to the eye – it sets the scene for the whole meal.
* Choose dishes that are simple for your guests to serve – individual portions look attractive, such as chicken fillets, fish steaks, or duck breasts in small amounts of sauce. Or individual portions that can be served en croute – for example, salmon en croute.
* Avoid grilled meat and poultry, which may dry out.
* Serve gratin or baked vegetable dishes, as these suffer less from being kept warm.
* If you are serving large joints of meat, whether hot or cold, you will need someone available at the buffet table to carve for your guests.

* Choose elegant desserts – either a single dessert if it is being served to guests at the table, or two or three choices if they are serving themselves from the buffet table. Crème brûlée, crème caramel, chocolate meringue nests with raspberries, glazed fruit tarts, and tiny rich tortes all work well.
* Consider serving hand-made chocolates or truffles with the coffee.
* Remember to include dishes that can be enjoyed by those who have special diets.

CHAPTER 8
PICNICS

Summer picnics were once grand affairs favoured by the gentry . . . but they seem to have lost some of their style down the years. We may not have the services of a chauffeur-cum-butler to do the honours, but that doesn't mean we have to settle for soggy sandwiches, fizzy pop and stale tea.

What could be nicer than relaxing with friends or family enjoying a stylish but simple meal at a favourite country location, your local park, a concert, or a day at the races?

Yes, picnics do need a little planning, but with a bit of effort they can become special occasions. And the great thing is that they work well whether you've invited two guests or twenty.

Presentation is the key. Resist the temptation to plonk a motley collection of plastic containers on the tablecloth and invite your guests to 'tuck in'. Make it special and, unless it's a quick refuelling stop on a cross-country walk or you're likely to have to park your car away from the picnic spot, use china plates and cups, 'real' glasses and proper cutlery (obviously not your very best!). They're so much nicer than throwaway paper plates and plastic glasses, but admittedly far heavier. Use baskets for bread, crisps, savoury nibbles and fruit.

Take a white tablecloth and napkins. If you plan to have your picnic on the grass take along a blanket to put under the tablecloth and provide a firmer base. Remember blankets to sit on – and chairs if you have any elderly guests.

You don't need expensive wicker hampers to carry your picnic equipment – a sturdy cardboard box will do. But a cooler box or a sturdy cooler bag is essential to keep food cold, fresh and uncrushed.

Anthea's top tip

I love using Kilner jars for picnics. They come in a variety of sizes and are perfect for carrying everything from the pickles to the biscuits and sweets. But they are weighty so you'll need to use your car as a 'larder' or use lighter alternatives if you have to carry your picnic.

The location

If you are planning a picnic in the countryside, check out your location in advance – you don't want to end up leading a convoy of cars along country lanes looking for a suitable spot. It's also a good idea to check whether there are any toilet facilities nearby. If there are young children at the picnic avoid fast-flowing rivers and lakes for safety reasons.

The food

Whether you are serving an array of savoury and sweet goodies, or simply some crusty bread, a selection of cheeses and fruit, accompanied by a nice bottle of chilled white wine, every picnic can be special.

Ideal picnic foods include:

* Cold meats (try to make them interesting – stuffed loin of pork, home-roasted ham, spicy chicken fillets)
* Smoked trout and salmon
* Savoury pies
* Flans and savoury tarts (choose some suitable for vegetarian guests)
* Dips and crudités
* Pâtés and crisp Melba toasts
* An interesting cheeseboard with grapes, figs and pears

More picnic ideas:

* Make salads with items that can be eaten individually – leaves of little gem lettuces, sprigs of lamb's lettuce, radishes, cherry tomatoes, pepper strips, celery, chicory leaves, cucumber batons, baby corn and trimmed sugar-snap peas. Provide a mayonnaise for dipping and a classic French dressing separately.
* New potato salad and jewelled rice salad also travel well, as does a home-made coleslaw made with interesting ingredients such as red and white cabbage, thinly sliced fennel, onion, thickly grated carrot and thinly sliced rings of radish. Throw in some sultanas, and unsalted peanuts to provide extra crunch, and dress with a French dressing or mayonnaise.
* Fill a breadbasket with a range of interesting breads and rolls – tomato and olive, walnut, seeded, rustic granary, ciabatta. Remember to take along butter in the cool box.

Sandwiches:

- There is a place for sandwiches at a stylish picnic but try something more imaginative than humble cheese and pickle on floppy white bread. To give them a sense of occasion, wrap in greaseproof paper, tie with string and attach a 'parcel' label to them.

Try these:

- Thin strips of roast turkey, thinly sliced Gruyère cheese, wholegrain mustard, thinly sliced tomato and crisp lettuce. (Line the sandwich with the lettuce and remove the seeds from the tomato.)
- Small pieces of smoked salmon, a squeeze of lemon, thinly sliced cucumber, a few capers and a sprig of dill.
- Succulent sliced roast beef with horseradish butter.
- Baby salad leaves, blue cheese and chopped walnuts.
- Moist roast ham, Brie and pineapple.

Keep desserts simple and easy to transport – something that can be packed in individual containers. Beautifully iced 'grown-up' cupcakes make a popular dessert, as do fresh strawberries and cream. A cheeseboard and fruit are always welcome.

Drinks

Have coffee and tea (take milk and sugar separately), some cold drinks and water. The packs of single-serving drip-through coffee are great for picnics.

If you take wine, remember that some of your guests may need to drive, so you'll need something nonalcoholic for them. Old-fashioned home-made lemonade or a refreshing fruit cooler are delicious alternatives and quick and easy to make.

New potato salad
(Serves 8 to 10)

1kg (about 2lb) baby new potatoes in their skins
2tbsp olive oil
1tbsp balsamic vinegar
1tbsp finely chopped fresh mint

Boil the potatoes until just tender, and drain. Combine the olive oil, vinegar and mint in a small basin and immediately pour over the potatoes. Toss gently and allow to cool in the fridge. Allow them to get cold before packing them.

Jewelled rice salad
(Serves 8 to 10)

500g (about 1lb) cold boiled long-grain or basmati rice
1 large red pepper, finely chopped
6 spring onions, sliced into thin rings
3 pineapple rings, chopped into small wedges
150g/5oz cold cooked frozen peas
Small tin of sweet corn, drained
A handful of slivered almonds (optional)
A handful of sultanas (optional)
Mayonnaise or French dressing

Place the rice in a bowl, add the vegetables and fruit and gently mix together. Lightly dress with mayonnaise or a French dressing.

Off the shelf

If you are short of time you can buy all the 'makings' for a sophisticated picnic from your local deli or supermarket. Then all you have to do is take care of the presentation. Remember to remove every scrap of packaging if you want to keep your picnic's origin a secret!

Who could resist this off-the-shelf picnic menu?

❧ Picnic Menu ❧

Smoked salmon on a bed of watercress served with lemon wedges and thin buttered brown bread triangles

Or

Duck and cranberry pâté with Melba toasts

───

Asparagus quiche
Game pie
Cold meat platter
Pickles and salsa
A selection of sandwiches

───

Mixed green salad
Marinated roasted vegetables
Fruity coleslaw
A selection of bread and rolls

───

Strawberries and cream
Lemon torte

───

Cheese and biscuits with grapes and figs
Coffee and truffles

Old-fashioned lemonade
(Makes 6 to 8 glasses)

4 lemons
175g/6oz caster sugar
600ml/20fl oz boiling water
600ml/20fl oz cold water

Squeeze the lemons and cut the skins into chunks. Place the juice and lemon skins into a bowl with the sugar. Add the boiling water and stir to dissolve the sugar. Leave the lemonade to cool in the fridge for about 4 hours. Strain into a jug and top up with the cold water. (If the lemonade is too sour for your taste, dissolve a little more sugar in a small quantity of water and add to the jug.)

Cranberry and raspberry cooler
A cool and refreshing summer drink
(Serves 8)

Combine 1 litre of cranberry and raspberry juice with the juice of one lemon and top up with sparkling water or white wine to taste. Float a few raspberries and mint leaves on the top. Serve over ice cubes with a raspberry frozen in the centre.

Picnic checklist

- Cutlery
- China
- Cups and glasses
- Serving spoons
- A sharp knife
- A corkscrew/bottle opener
- Salt and pepper
- Plenty of wet wipes for sticky fingers
- Napkins
- Blankets to sit on
- Some empty plastic bags to take all your rubbish home
- First-aid kit

Picnic tips

- If you are taking wine on your picnic, tape a corkscrew to a bottle before you leave home.
- Arrange salads in bowls and place in lidded containers to prevent them from getting crushed.
- Take salad dressings in screw-top containers and dress salad just before serving, or let your guests help themselves.
- Wrap glasses in bubble wrap to prevent breakages.
- Before you leave home place two folded napkins on each plate before you stack them, so there's no chance of you forgetting the napkins. Take along some spares.
- Keep all of your prepared food in the fridge and load it into your cooler boxes just before you leave. Remember the ice packs.
- A roll of kitchen towel is useful for wiping up spills.

A family picnic

Children love a sense of occasion, so make family picnics special too. Let the children help with the preparation.

Keep all of the food small – small sandwiches, little sausage rolls, mini meatballs, quiche cut into miniature wedges, pizza fingers, tiny decorated fairy cakes baked in sweet-cases. Make a mild cheese-and-yogurt dip and take along strips of pepper, cucumber, carrot and oven-baked crisps to dip.

For dessert make individual fruit-filled jellies or fruit desserts in ramekins, or dip the tips of strawberries in melted milk or white chocolate and put them in covered pots.

Give everyone their own individual picnic – pack the food into a gift bag or box from a card shop. Children will love the excitement of opening their own box or bag to discover what's inside.

Avoid bought fizzy drinks and serve a 'kids' own' fruit cooler – combine a carton of orange juice with a carton of raspberry juice and top up with water. To make it really special hang a few grapes or orange and cucumber slices over the rim of the glasses.

CHAPTER 9
BARBECUES

The moment the sun shines our thoughts turn to barbecues. They're fun and great for getting family and friends together . . . but don't let anyone tell you they just happen. They take planning if you want to sail through looking as cool as the proverbial cucumber.

The only thing you won't be able to plan is the British weather! So have a Plan B up your sleeve. (When you send out your invitations let your guests know there is a Plan B so if the heavens open on the day of the party, they won't assume the event has been cancelled and leave you to eat a mountain of chicken, burgers and salads for the next week!)

Now for the preparation. The garden first – whether it's large or small it must be neat and tidy. Mow the lawn, sweep the patio, hide the bins out of sight, and clear away toys and garden clutter. If the party is going on into the evening invest in some garden lights or candles – they really do make even the smallest garden or courtyard look magical. Remember to drape some wraps over the chairs for your female guests in case it gets chilly as the sun goes down.

Gather up as many chairs, benches and tables as you can. If you're short of chairs, put some blankets and cushions on the patio. You will need at least one or two sturdy tables for the food, and somewhere comfortable for any elderly guests to sit. If you regularly eat outside why not buy a garden canopy? You can get them for as little as £15 – they do keep off the sun and can cope with a light shower.

Barbecue tips

- If you are using a charcoal-burning barbecue allow heating-up time. Charcoal is ready to cook on when at least 80 per cent of the coals are covered with grey ash.
- Place your barbecue away from the main party area, and well away from fences, shrubs, trees – or the neighbour's back door. Position it side on to the wind on a firm, flat surface.
- Never use anything other than fire lighters or commercial barbecue lighting products to get the charcoal burning.
- If you can, invest in a gas or electric barbecue – they're brilliant and life's too short to spend it blowing on coals!
- Enlist help with 'barbecue minding' if possible – it's one of those 'alpha male' things so you shouldn't be short of volunteers if there are men around.

The food

Provide some crudités and dips, small Spanish tapas or Greek meze dishes for your guests to eat while the food is sizzling on the barbecue – it takes the pressure off the cook. You can find tapas and meze dishes in good delis and supermarket chiller counters if you don't want to make them yourself. Bottled roasted vegetables, olives, and sun-dried roasted peppers and tomatoes make ideal tapas.

If your barbecue is small, just cook a few items on it, and prepare the rest of the food in the oven and whisk it to the table at the last minute. (Marinate meat in a smoky-tasting marinade and few of your guests will notice the difference.)

If you can, have your food on one table and your drinks on another. Cover your tables with attractive tablecloths. Remember to have plenty of paper napkins for sticky fingers.

Keep the food simple. You only need two or three meat items, and perhaps some juicy king prawns and sweet pepper, mushroom and onion kebabs to pop on at the last minute. Chicken, steak, pork and lamb chops

Anthea's top tip

Slices of French bread drizzled with olive oil and wrapped in foil – shiny side in – and popped on the barbecue are delicious.

are perfect on the barbecue, as well as home-made or good-quality bought beefburgers, and sausages – essential if you have young children among your guests. Remember to allow extra cooking time if your meat has the bone in.

Salmon steaks, tuna steaks and trout are also delicious, but you need to keep your eye on them, as fish can quickly become overcooked and dry.

For extra flavour and to keep your food moist, marinate meat and fish before cooking. Make your own marinade or use one of the wide variety available from the supermarket.

To save time ask your butcher to prepare and marinate a selection of meat for you. Then all you have to do is collect it and cook it.

Vegetarians are often forgotten at barbecues, so always have a suitable vegetarian dish on your food table.

Add a couple of colourful salads, a bowl of warm baby new potatoes (try them tossed in chopped mint and olive oil) or some small baked jacket potatoes, and wedges of crusty bread, and you'll have a summer feast.

Finish with a fresh fruit salad or use the remaining heat from the barbecue to serve the classic barbecue favourite – baked bananas in their skins with ice cream and a drizzle of maple syrup or rum. Or try grilled pineapple wedges – cut a fresh pineapple into six wedges lengthways and grill on the barbecue, or sprinkle wedges with soft brown sugar, douse with rum, wrap in a foil parcel and grill. Summer fruits in foil parcels are also a sumptuous ending to a barbecue party.

Off the shelf
If you are short of time check out the supermarket and deli for:
- Ready-marinated fish and meat
- Pickles, sun-dried tomatoes and roasted marinated vegetables
- Ready-prepared salad leaves
- Tapas and meze dishes
- Assorted breads and rolls

Drinks

Serve wine, cooling fruit punches and spritzers to drink both at daytime and evening barbecues. You will often find at daytime barbecues that many people will opt for soft drinks rather than wine. Serve a variety of soft drinks and mineral water.

Drinks tips

* Freeze small pieces of lemon, lime, orange, cucumber, grapes or red berries in ice cubes, to drop into fresh juice drinks.
* If you are serving an iced fruit punch, freeze some of the fruit juice you are incorporating in ice-cube trays – they won't dilute the punch.
* Make a simple and inexpensive drinks cooler from a large coloured lidded plastic bin from the DIY store. Fill it with ice (you can buy it from any supermarket or off-licence) and add your bottles and cans.

Sparkling summer punch
(Serves 10–12)

1 bottle white wine
1 bottle Champagne or sparkling wine
120ml/4fl oz Vodka
Rind of 2 oranges, finely sliced
1 tin apricot halves
Ice

Chill the wine. Steep the orange rind in the vodka for a few hours. Then strain the vodka into a large glass bowl or punch bowl. Discard the orange rind. Just before you are ready to serve add the apricots, the sweet white wine and the sparkling wine to the vodka. Serve in tall glasses, a quarter filled with ice. Add an apricot to each glass as you serve.

- My favourite barbecue drink is Pimm's – but it must have nectarines in it! Delicious!
- If you've got a birthday coming up, ask for a chiminea or a fire bowl – they give off a lovely log-burning smell.
- If you are serving a spritzer, drop a few frozen grapes into the glass. They keep the drink cool, and reduce the amount of drink in the glasses.

Summer fruit punch
(Serves 10)

600ml/1 pint mango juice
600ml/1 pint pineapple juice
600ml/1 pint apple juice
Sparkling mineral water
1 red eating apple, cut into wedges
1 orange, thinly sliced
1 lemon, thinly sliced
A few strawberries or seedless grapes

Pour the fruit juices into a large jug or punchbowl and add sparkling mineral water to taste. (If it is too sweet, add the juice of a lemon or orange.) Add the fruit. Serve in straight-sided glasses over ice.

White wine spritzer
(Serves 12 to 16)

2 bottles chilled white wine
1 litre sparkling mineral water or soda water
1kg seedless white grapes or white currants, washed and frozen

Combine the chilled wine, mineral or soda water and frozen grapes or white currants in a large jug. Add ice cubes. For a change add lemon or orange ice cubes to the spritzer. Slice a lemon and an orange and cut each slice into quarters. Place a quarter in each of the sections of an ice cube tray and top up with sparkling mineral water. Freeze until ready to use.

More barbecue tips
- Wipe over the grill of your barbecue with oil before lighting it – it will help prevent food sticking.
- Grease stains on the patio can be removed by covering them with clay cat litter. Grind it in with your foot, leave it until the next morning and sweep it away.
- It's simpler to cook jacket potatoes in the oven rather than on the barbecue. Rub them in olive oil and sea salt and bake until they are tender.
- Boiling sausages for five minutes before putting them on the barbecue will help prevent them charring before the inside is cooked.
- Keep food covered to protect it from insects and dust. Try burning citronella candles to keep bugs at bay but have some insect repellent and after-bite cream ready, just in case.

Marinades and bastes

Marinate meat for two to four hours in any of these tasty recipes:

* Hot lime and ginger – combine the grated rind and juice of a lime, a teaspoon of finely chopped ginger, a small red chilli finely chopped and a small pot of natural yogurt.
* Sweet chilli – combine one tablespoon of sweet chilli sauce, two tablespoons of olive oil and two spring onions, finely chopped.
* Sweet garlic and mustard – combine a crushed clove of garlic, two tablespoons of olive oil, one tablespoon of Dijon mustard and a tablespoon of honey.

Brush meat while it is on the barbecue with one of these:

* Sweet chilli glaze – combine a tablespoon of honey with three tablespoons of oil, a tablespoon of balsamic vinegar and a pinch of chilli flakes.
* Mustard and tomato – combine two tablespoons of olive oil, two tablespoons of tomato ketchup and two tablespoons of wholegrain mustard.
* Lime and honey – combine three tablespoons of olive oil, two tablespoons of lime juice and a teaspoon of runny honey.

Seven sizzling skewers

Kebabs are always popular. Thread the food to be cooked onto metal or wooden skewers and brush with a baste or marinade – or just oil. (If you use wooden skewers remember to soak them in water for about an hour so they don't burn.) Try these combinations:

* Chunks of lamb (marinated in olive oil and fresh thyme), red pepper and onion wedges
* Chunks of sausage, button mushrooms, rolled-up bacon and cherry tomatoes
* Chunks of gammon steak, pineapple, baby sweet corn and cherry tomatoes
* Chunks of halloumi cheese, courgette rings, onion wedges and baby plum tomatoes
* King prawns (marinated in oil, lemon juice, crushed garlic and chopped parsley), lemon wedges and cherry tomatoes
* Chunks of aubergine, red pepper, courgette rings, onion wedges and plum tomatoes
* Chunks of chicken, pineapple, mushroom, cherry tomatoes and onion wedges

Italian panzanella salad

(Serves 8)

20 baby plum tomatoes, halved
4 garlic cloves, finely chopped
8 thick slices of ciabatta bread (slightly stale)
2 medium red onions, chopped
20cm cucumber, deseeded and thinly sliced diagonally
2tbsp flat-leaf parsley, chopped
4tbsp capers in brine, drained
12 green olives, halved (optional)
A handful of basil leaves, torn
For the dressing:
3tbsp cider vinegar or white wine vinegar
8tbsp extra-virgin olive oil
1tbsp balsamic vinegar
Coarse sea salt
Freshly ground black pepper

1. Preheat the oven to 180°C/Gas 4.
2. Arrange the tomato halves on a nonstick baking tray and sprinkle with the chopped garlic. Bake for 30 to 35 minutes until the tomato is soft and some of the juices have evaporated. (If the tomatoes are cooking too quickly reduce the heat a little. They should not be charred.) Set aside to cool.
3. Lightly oil a stovetop ridged griddle and lightly toast the slices of ciabatta. When the toast is cool, roughly tear into bite-sized pieces. Place into a large bowl and add the tomatoes, onion, cucumber slices, parsley and drained capers, and olives, if using. Season with salt and pepper. Combine the dressing ingredients and sprinkle over the salad. Leave for an hour to give the flavours time to develop. Add the torn basil leaves and serve.

Simple 'real' beefburgers
(Makes 10)

800g/1lb 12oz lean minced beef
1 egg, beaten
2 garlic cloves, crushed
2 shallots, finely chopped
2tbsp parsley, chopped
2tbsp Worcestershire sauce
A pinch of chilli flakes (optional)
Salt and freshly ground black pepper

Place all the ingredients in a large bowl and mix together with your hands until thoroughly combined. Shape into 10 burgers and place in the fridge for at least an hour or until needed.

Note: For herby beefburgers omit the Worcestershire sauce and chilli flakes and replace with a tablespoon of chopped fresh parsley and a teaspoon of fresh thyme.

Honey and garlic chicken
(Serves 10)

10 pieces of chicken
For the marinade:
2tbsp white wine vinegar
2tbsp lemon juice
2tbsp honey
12tbsp olive oil
2 cloves garlic

Combine the marinade ingredients in a small bowl. Place the chicken in a shallow dish and pour over the marinade. Cover and chill for 2 to 4 hours. Cook on the barbecue or in an oven until the chicken is thoroughly cooked.

Baked fruit parcels
(Serves 10)

10 nectarines, stoned and sliced
350g/12oz raspberries
450g/1lb blueberries
Juice of 3 small oranges
2tsp ground cinnamon
4tbsp caster sugar
To serve:
3tbsp toasted flaked almonds
Natural yogurt or fromage frais

1. Prepare the fruit and place in a bowl. Pour over the orange juice. Sprinkle over the sugar and cinnamon. Take 10 large pieces of foil and place some fruit in the centre of each piece. Fold the foil to enclose the fruit in a parcel.
2. Place the parcels onto a medium-hot barbecue and bake for 5 minutes. Remove the parcels from the barbecue and carefully transfer the fruit and the juices into individual serving bowls.
3. Top with yogurt or fromage frais and sprinkle over the flaked almonds. Serve immediately.

Celery, apple and hazelnut salad
(Serves 6–8)

1 large head celery
4 red apples, washed
1 yogurt pot of hazelnuts, lightly toasted
1/4 yogurt pot of good quality mayonnaise
1 carton natural yogurt
Juice of half a lemon
Freshly ground black pepper

1. Finely slice the celery. Core and chop the apples – but don't remove the skin. Put into a bowl. Add the hazelnuts.
2. Combine the yogurt, mayonnaise and lemon juice in a small bowl and add to the celery, apples and hazelnuts. Season with pepper, stir together and transfer to a serving bowl lined with lettuce leaves.

Safety

- Keep young children well away from the barbecue.
- Use long-handled tools, and wear protective gloves when using a barbecue.
- Keep uncooked and cooked food separate. Bring uncooked food to the barbecue in lidded plastic boxes just before you are ready to cook it.
- Have a bowl of water and a towel handy for hand-washing before and after you touch raw meat and fish.
- Never leave your barbecue unattended. Have everything you need on a side table so you don't have to keep dashing back to the kitchen.
- Always wear an apron, and avoid voluminous sleeves if you are tending a barbecue.

. . . something different

Send invitations to friends – along with a map grid reference, or written directions, to a beauty spot or a deserted cove – inviting them to an early-morning breakfast barbecue. Arrive ahead of your guests with a simple feast and wait for them to find you.

All you need is a couple of disposable barbecues, some luxury sausages and bacon, a pile of buttered rolls of different kinds, a bowl of assorted fruit, coffee and, of course, buck's fizz.

Don't forget blankets to sit on. Many beauty spots even have picnic tables so all you need to do is add a tablecloth and lay the table. Remember to check that barbecues are allowed and avoid areas where you might disturb the neighbours.

CHAPTER 10
EVENINGS IN

Inviting girlfriends around for an 'evening in' is a great chance for everyone to catch up with the gossip and relax, watch a movie and try out some new make-up or pampering treatments.

No one will be expecting you to serve up a gourmet feast, just some simple food that is either quick to prepare, or can be made in advance. If you're dashing home from work and likely to be short of time, no one will mind if you cheat a little by buying some of the food and giving it a home-made look.

A single dish is all that you need – this is a good time to have a go at all those 'bung-everything-into-the-oven' dishes we see TV chefs creating. Make an interesting salad, warm some wedges of crusty bread to mop up the juices and the job is done. If you want to serve a dessert keep it simple – a bowl of strawberries and cream or a platter of exotic fruits and a fromage frais dip are delicious.

But you don't always have to cook. Simply serve wine and some crostini with a variety of toppings, or a couple of plates of canapés and a delicious dessert.

If you want to cook ahead you could make:

* A tasty chilli
* A curry
* A spicy Cajun or jerk chicken

If you think your guests would fancy something lighter try:

* A pasta dish
* A risotto
* A speedy oven-cooked 'all in together' chicken or fish dish
* A main-meal salad
* A quick cauliflower and broccoli cheese with crispy bacon and Parmesan topping and a salad
* A potato wedges bowl – bowl food that can be eaten easily with a fork is great if you plan to sit around with your feet up watching movies

Rustic baked garlic chicken
(Serves 4)

4 chicken breasts, lightly brushed with olive oil
4 individual portions garlic and herb cheese
2tsp olive oil
2 small courgettes cut into chunks
1 red onion cut into wedges
4 sprigs thyme
1 large clove garlic, sliced
1 red pepper, deseeded and cut into large chunks
1 yellow pepper, deseeded and cut into large chunks
Salt and freshly ground black pepper
16 cherry or baby plum tomatoes
10 black olives (optional)

1. Preheat the oven to 180C/Gas 4.
2. Make a deep slit in the side of the chicken breasts and insert a portion of garlic
   and herb cheese in each. Place on a large oiled ovenproof dish or baking tray
   (use 1 teaspoon of the oil).
3. Place the thyme, garlic, red onion wedges, courgette, red and yellow peppers
   in a bowl, add the remaining teaspoon of olive oil and toss to lightly coat the
   vegetables in oil. Arrange around the chicken breasts. Season with the salt and
   freshly ground black pepper.
4. Put the dish in the oven and bake for 15 minutes. Add the tomatoes and olives,
   if used, to the pan and cook for a further 10 to 15 minutes or until the chicken is
   cooked through. Serve with a large salad.

Hot spicy wedgie bowls
(Serves 4)

1. Buy some frozen or chilled spicy potato wedges and cook according to the
   instructions on the packet.
2. Chop 6 thin slices of cooked ham into strips. Grate 175g (6 oz) of mature
   Cheddar. Finely chop 3 spring onions and one small chilli.

3. Pile the cooked potato wedges in the bottom and around the edge of 4 bowls, add the ham, sprinkle over the cheese and the chopped chilli. Grill until the cheese is melted and bubbling. Sprinkle over the spring onion and serve with a salad for everyone to dip into.

* Alternatively, line the bowl with cooked potato wedges, add a drained tin of tuna or salmon, top with cheese and grill. Garnish with tomato slices or halved cherry tomatoes and a sprig of parsley.

Lisa's chilli con carne
(Serves 4)

800g/1lb 12oz lean mince
1tbsp extra-virgin olive oil
2 tins chopped tomatoes
1 sachet of chilli con carne mix
1 green pepper (cut into strips to suit)
1 punnet of small mushrooms (cut into quarters)
2 tins of kidney beans in chilli sauce
1 large red onion (sliced)
½ clove of garlic
4 small cups of basmati rice
Grated cheese (strength to suit taste)
Bag of tortilla chips
1 pot of guacamole dip
1 pot of sour cream dip
1 pot of salsa dip

1. Heat the olive oil in a large frying pan or saucepan. Add the mince and cook on a low heat until brown, then drain off any fat. Stir in the chopped tomatoes and chilli con carne mix. Add the kidney beans in chilli sauce, green pepper, mushrooms, onion and crushed garlic. Cook over a moderate heat for 15 to 20 minutes, stirring occasionally.
2. Meanwhile cook the rice according to the packet instructions. Rinse through with boiling water (this helps to stop the rice sticking).
3. Serve with rice and/or tortilla chips sprinkled with cheese and placed under the grill to melt. Serve with the Italian flag – sour cream, salsa and guacamole dips!

Apricot crème
(Serves 4)

1 large tin skinned apricots
A miniature of apricot or peach brandy
250g/9oz tub of crème fraîche or fromage frais
Dark muscovado sugar to decorate
8 mint leaves

Drain the apricots, and cut into pieces. Place in the bottom of small wine glasses. Drizzle over the liqueur. Top with crème fraîche or fromage frais. Level the top and sprinkle over a heaped teaspoon of dark brown sugar. Chill in the fridge for 2 hours. (The sugar will melt, forming a delicious dark layer.) Before serving decorate with the mint leaves.

Chocolate, banana and raspberry sundae
Try this pure indulgence for a girlie night in watching DVDs!
(Makes 4)

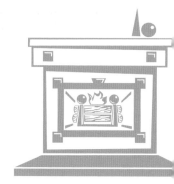

3 small bananas, cut into slices
150g/6oz fresh raspberries
8 scoops of the most decadent chocolate ice cream you can find
4 scoops good quality vanilla ice cream
4 tbsp 'real' chocolate sauce
Chocolate curls or slivered almonds
150ml/5fl oz double cream

1. Place the cream in a clean, dry bowl and lightly whip.
2. Take 4 sundae glasses or tall glasses and layer the ice cream, fruit and chocolate sauce into the glasses. Top with the cream and the chocolate curls or slivered almonds.
3. To make chocolate curls use a vegetable peeler. Make them on to a piece of kitchen towel so that you can easily lift them into the sundaes. Picking the curls up with your fingers will cause them to melt.

Ring the changes: try fresh cherries or strawberries instead of the raspberries.

Have a Movie Night for the girls

- Hire some chick flicks and get in some wine and chocolates
- Heart-throbs Night – show films featuring your favourite actor
- 007 Night – show your favourite James Bond movies – and serve Martinis (shaken, not stirred, of course!) and savoury nibbles

If you don't fancy cooking for a Movie Night:

- Get in a takeaway and eat it out of the boxes
- Serve giant paper cups filled with popcorn, along with marshmallows and ice cream

Have a 'Party Plan' girlie night

Get in an organiser who runs 'home parties' for one of the large companies – for example Avon, Body Shop, Virgin Vie, Anne Summers – and invite the girls round.

Party-plan organisers often advertise in local newspapers but you can also check out the company websites. You'll find details in the resources section at the back of the book. The websites will tell you about the different kinds of parties, what you will need to provide and what you will receive in return for hosting a party in your home.

Serve some savoury or sweet nibbles and chilled white wine. Or if it's a summer 'do', elderflower wine, Pimm's or ginger beer are great for a change.

CHAPTER 11
CHILDREN'S PARTIES

Organising parties for children may seem a daunting prospect – but it's great fun and well worth all the effort.

But try not to get caught up in a pointless game of one-upmanship. Aim to give your child a party they will really love. Children's parties are an area where peer pressure can rear its ugly head – and sadly it comes not only from other children but from other parents as they try to outdo each other by holding the biggest, grandest, most spectacular party with the largest 'goody bags' (more about those later!). Resolve not to travel along that road.

Planning the party

Where?

Decide which rooms you are going to use – if it's summer try to make use of the garden. Remember small children will need more space to run around than older ones.

If you haven't got room at home consider hiring a venue, although it will increase the cost considerably and you'll need to transport everything. Or look in your local directory for one of the scores of places, like zoos, play zones, adventure parks, ceramic studios and restaurant chains that host children's parties. This is becoming a very popular option with children.

When?

Whether you hold the party after school or at the weekend, keep it short – two or three hours will be quite long enough for young children . . . and for you. Always enlist as much adult help as you can.

How many guests?

Be realistic when deciding how many young guests you have space for. Don't be badgered into inviting the whole class. Unless you've got the stamina of a marathon runner – and a lot of help – six to eight children is a realistic number for a party at home.

Invitations

Send out the invitations two or three weeks in advance and get definite acceptances (so there's time to send out other invitations to make up the numbers). Try to be inventive with your invitations.

- Tie them to balloons and write the party guest's name on the balloon using a permanent marker pen.
- Make a gingerbread person with a hole through it and attach a coloured luggage label with all the party details on.

What kind of party?

This will depend on the age of the party child and their interests. If they are old enough, let them be involved in helping to find a theme for their party.

Pre-school

For pre-school children you're probably best theming the party around familiar TV characters or the latest Disney favourites.

Parties in the garden are ideal for children of this age group as they are too young to take part in organised games. Clear a large space and let them play with a selection of outdoor toys.

Many parents like to stay with their little ones at this age – and you'll be grateful for their help – so be ready with some nice cakes and cups of tea.

Four to eight

At this age children are incredibly active so parties for them are best planned with almost military precision. Make a plan of games to play both before and after tea. Remember to have any little prizes that you will need ready. If you can get them out into the garden to play games, so much the better.

Hiring an entertainer for this age group is often a good idea – a clown, a magician or a face-painter – but keep their 'performances' short, as attention spans can be limited.

Eight to twelve

By this age children have very definite ideas, and what is 'cool' this week could be very definitely 'uncool' the next. So getting them involved in planning the party and deciding what kind of entertainment they want is the route to success.

This is the age when they like to be 'doing' things so bear this in mind when you are planning the party. They may prefer to go out to the cinema, ice rink or bowling alley with a few friends, followed by a pizza. If you do take them out for a birthday treat, make sure that you have a couple of friends with you to help, and do not leave the children alone. If they are at a restaurant, and you feel they are responsible, let them have a little privacy. Sit with your friends at a nearby table so you can keep an eye on the proceedings.

Party teas

Keep the food small and familiar. This isn't the time to be inventive with sandwich fillings, so don't offer too much choice:

- Two kinds of sandwiches – choose from Marmite, ham, chicken, peanut butter, cheese.
- Two savoury items – from cocktail sausages, home-made mini burgers (use a pastry cutter to cut mini burger rolls from bridge rolls), home-made pizza squares, oven-roasted crisps.
- Two cakes – how about gingerbread people, home-made small cookies, iced biscuits, decorated cupcakes made in sweet cases.
- One dessert – a few ideas include a fruit jelly, tiny individual ice-cream dessert, individual tubs of ice cream served in a large bowl of ice.
- A bowl of veggie sticks and fruit – carrot, cucumber, cherry tomatoes, grapes, apple wedges, strawberries. Cut cherry tomatoes, grapes and strawberries in half to avoid anyone choking.
- Avoid fizzy drinks. Instead serve diluted fresh fruit juice and water.

As children get older they will have their own ideas of what makes the best party tea. Be guided by them – within reason!

Party tea tips and hints

- Try to make all of your party food from scratch. That way you can avoid the E numbers, artificial flavourings, colourings and excess sugar so often found in 'ready-made' food targeted at children.
- Put two or three plates of the same food on the table – it'll avoid table climbing if they can all reach everything!
- For young partygoers use disposable or wipe-clean tablecloths and shatterproof plates and tumblers. If you're worried about drinks being spilled give the children cartons of juice with straws.
- Start with the savoury items and keep the dessert and the birthday cake off the table until later.
- Have plenty of wet wipes for sticky fingers and faces.

The birthday cake

Birthday cakes are a 'must have' – you have to have somewhere to put the candles, even if the cake isn't eaten by all of the guests! Unless you are an inventive cake maker you don't need to make the cake yourself. There is a wide range available at the supermarkets and at local bakers. Or you may have a fantastic cake creator among your friends who'd love the challenge of providing something extra special.

As an alternative to a single cake make a tower of beautifully iced cupcakes with the names of the young guests iced on some of the cakes, and the candles placed on others. Then they can take their own 'named' cake home with them.

Party food boxes

Children love opening boxes – it feels like a present. So as a change from the traditional party spread why not try serving the party tea in pretty individual food boxes? You'll find a selection of party boxes at all good party suppliers.

Always . . .

- Make sure you ask parents if their children have any allergies, and if there are any foods they are not permitted to eat.
- Take a phone number from the parents of each child when they drop them off at the party, so you can contact them in case of an emergency. (There are also times when children, particularly young ones, decide that they just want to go home.)
- Have a supply of plasters and antiseptic wipes on hand for bumps and grazes.

If you have sweets at a party, portion them out into individual pretty bags rather than putting out a large bowl and letting the children help themselves. It makes them look special and prevents anyone eating too many!

Party themes

Children love parties with themes. It really takes the excitement levels up a few notches. Choose a theme that reflects your child's interests.

Here are a few ideas to get you thinking:

Pre-teens Oscars party

Roll out a red carpet for a party little girls will never forget. Award 'Oscars' for funny categories – the 'star' with the snazziest shoes, for example. Ask friends with cameras to be 'paparazzi' to snap the children when they arrive. Put on an up-to-the-minute DVD and let them eat popcorn from mini paper cones, veggie sticks and cookies while they're watching it.

Make the climax of the event a glamorous gala tea with an awards ceremony – they'll love every minute of it. If you can, construct a raised podium for them to climb in true Hollywood fashion to collect their awards.

Serve pasta with a home-made sauce and a crisp green salad, or chicken drumsticks with home-made barbecue sauce, tiny jacket potatoes and a salad. Finish with a mini ice cream and fruit sundae. Don't forget the 'fawn's fizz' – freshly squeezed orange juice topped up with mineral water and for good measure a thin slice of orange slipped over the rim of the glass. Serve the fizz in plastic wine glasses for that grown-up feel.

Halloween party

Children love dressing up and Halloween parties give them a perfect excuse to become witches, wizards and ghosts. They'll have hours of fun helping to create their costumes, but if time is short the supermarkets are filled with inexpensive masks, witchy wigs and costumes during October. Letting the children have a Halloween party is a good way of heading off pleas to go trick or treating – and far safer.

Turn your party room into a witch's cavern. Decorate it with spiders made from fluffy pipe cleaners and fluffy balls from the craft shop, replace a couple of light bulbs with orange or green ones to give the room an eerie glow, paint faces on black balloons, attach

the balloons to sticks and drape black cloth capes around them. Stand the sticks in sturdy containers around the room.

Serve some ghostly food:

● Beefburger spiders. Make tiny round beefburgers, cook them and stick Twiglets in the sides for legs. Make eyes with tiny blobs of cream cheese.

● Cut glacé cherries into quarters and stick on the end of chocolate finger biscuits with a little red icing (use a tube of ready-made icing) to make witch's fingers.

● Make tiny cupcakes in sweet cases and decorate with black and green icing spiders, bats and witch's cats.

Witches' broomsticks

(Makes 24)

Let the children join in the fun and make these quick and easy Halloween snacks.

1 packet ready rolled shortcrust pastry
50g/2oz Red Leicester cheese
50g/2oz mild Cheddar cheese
A little milk to glaze

1. Preheat the oven to 200°C/Gas 6.

2. Dust a pastry board or clean work surface with a little flour and lay out the pastry sheet. Cut in half. Cut strips of pastry 2½cm/1 inch wide along the shortest width of the pastry. Do the same with the other half. Make three 2cm/¾ inch long cuts at one end of each of the strips of pastry. Spread them out slightly to make a broom shape. Lay the 'brooms' on a sheet of baking parchment on a baking tray. Brush with milk and sprinkle the grated Red Leicester on half of the brooms and the grated Cheddar on the other half.

3. Bake for 10–12 minutes until they are crisp. Allow to cool on the tray for 15 minutes and then transfer to a cooling rack to get cold.

A Halloween game

Paint a large picture of a witch's head and mount it on a cork message board. Make sure your witch has an enormous nose. Blindfold each of the children in turn and give them a small blob of Blu-tack or Plasticine. They have to stick their 'warts' on the face of the witch. The child whose wart is nearest the end of the witch's nose is the winner.

Sleepover party

By the time they are eight most children are begging to be allowed to have their friends to stay for a 'sleepover' party. Saturday nights and school holidays are good times for sleepovers as there's no school next day. But don't expect to get an early night or a lie-in the next morning – excitement levels at sleepovers are notoriously high!

Sleeping in sleeping bags all together in one room is part of the fun, so ask the young guests to bring their sleeping bags, a pillow and a favourite toy. But keep the numbers down.

Serve a meal you know they will all enjoy at about six o'clock followed by a platter of fresh fruit slices and a yogurt-and-honey dip. Put on a favourite DVD – you'll probably need two, as they won't be planning on having an early night. Have an interval during the film and serve popcorn and diluted juice. After the film let them have a little time to play quietly before bedtime.

The highlight of every sleepover is a midnight feast, but don't worry, you don't need to wait that long if you can collect watches and mobile phones to 'put in a safe place' before they get into bed. They'll never know it isn't really midnight! For their 'midnight' feast you could give them hot chocolate or warm milk, cookies and fingers of toast with honey, peanut butter or Marmite. Then all you have to do is wait patiently for all the squeals, shrieks and giggles to subside as they gradually fall off to sleep.

'Cook in' parties

Boys and girls both love the chance to get into the kitchen for a good 'cook in'. Lay the table before they arrive and make it look special. Be ready with a pile of aprons for the trainee chefs. If you – or a friend – are handy with a sewing machine it's easy to run up some little aprons using inexpensive striped material or a white sheet from the charity shop. Get a bright fabric pen from a craft shop and write 'CHEF' on the bib. After the party they can take their aprons home with them.

Let them build their own pizza. Make some individual pizza bases in advance – you can use a ready mix – and have a selection of toppings, home-made tomato sauce and grated cheese ready for them to use. Then while the pizzas are cooking you could play a couple of food-themed games. Let them taste some unusual fruits and see if they can guess what they are.

Instead of making pizzas they could decorate cupcakes, or make some interesting sandwiches for tea.

A girlie makeover party

Collect together a box of glamorous accessories, feather boas, shawls, evening gloves, tiaras, jewellery, etc., and let the party girls 'glam up' and put on a fashion parade. Give them a box of make-up to complete the look – or have someone on hand to help.

A pirate party

Ask the guests to come as pirates, and theme the games – hunting for buried treasure, pirate statues, etc. Use your imagination and give the food a nautical theme and piratical names such as 'pirate ships' made from halved bridge rolls with sails made from triangles of cheese slices threaded on cocktail sticks, and tiny iced sponge cakes decorated to look like treasure chests.

A safari party

Paint some of the young guests' faces to resemble animals and gather up some inexpensive safari-style hats so the other guests can be park rangers. Give your food and games an animal theme.

A Wild West party

Little boys – and girls – still like cowboys, so why not ask them to come to the party dressed as cowboys and cowgirls and serve the food from an improvised 'chuck wagon' in best cowboy style. You could serve baby bangers and baked beans along with the usual party food.

   If you've got a large garden you might like to think about hiring a giant tepee or a bucking bronco.

Ceramics party

If you've got a ceramics studio near you that does parties, it's worth giving this a try if you have a group of young girls to entertain. They all get a chance to paint a mug or a plate, which they take home after the party.

Football crazy

Let the boys and their friends wear their favourite team's strip. Erect a goal in the garden and have a penalty-shooting competition and other football-themed games. Serve popular food available at football matches – they'll tell you what's the 'in thing'.

Harry Potter

If the party girl or boy is a fan of the young magician ask the guests to come dressed as witches and wizards. They'll love another chance to get out their Halloween costumes from last year. You could also hire a magician.

Jungle Book

This is a great excuse to hire a face painter or enlist the help of friends to paint the guests' faces to represent animals. Rename some of the popular party games to give them a jungle feel, such as 'animal statues' and 'pin the tail on the elephant'.

If you decide not to have a theme just give your home a party makeover. Balloons, streamers, fairy lights and party hats are all you need.

Teenage parties

These are always a difficult area and probably one best 'negotiated' with the teens. But whatever you do, however pitiful the pleadings, or sincere the promises, don't agree to leave them 'home alone' to party at this age. They may be thoroughly responsible but what about their guests, or – a more worrying prospect – gatecrashers?

When they're too old for party games and too young for the pub teenagers may welcome the suggestion of an outing to the cinema or ice rink followed by a pizza, or a session go-karting, paintball or laser with a group of friends. Remember to enlist some help with transport – don't overload the car; it's safer to hire a minibus with a qualified driver.

'Goody bags'

If a campaign was launched to end the tyranny of 'party bags' I wonder how many hard-pressed mums would rush to sign up? No longer is sending young ones home from a party clutching a balloon and a piece of cake considered enough. Over the years the expectations of little partygoers – and sadly, also, of some parents – have got higher and higher. Party bags are nothing short of emotional blackmail, and so many of us are playing the game, wracking our brains and spending a fortune to provide bigger and bigger party bags. If this goes on they'll soon be dragging plastic sacks full of goodies home.

A friend recently heard her daughter asking a prospective party guest to whom she had just excitedly handed over a birthday-party invitation, whether she would be able to come. 'It depends,' came the reply. 'What's your mum putting in the party bags?' And this was a seven-year-old! At another party a young guest had to leave early and her mother blithely asked the hostess if they could 'take their party bag, now'.

Aren't these two good reasons to turn the clock back?

Safety

Whenever you have a party at your home make sure that it is safe, and the garden is 'escape-proof'. Ensure that pools and ponds are securely covered or locked out of reach. Always make sure you have some adult help on hand, even if there are only a small number of children at the party.

Cupcakes

Cupcakes are perfect for children's parties. They are just the right size, are quick and simple to make, and with a little imagination can be decorated to fit almost any party theme.

Here's a basic recipe and a few ideas.

To make 16 cup cakes

125g/4½oz caster sugar
125g/4½oz softened butter or margarine
2 medium eggs
125g/4½oz self-raising flour
1 level tsp baking powder
A few drops of vanilla extract
16 small paper cake cases

1. Preheat the oven to 190°C/Gas 5.
2. Put all of the ingredients into a bowl and whisk until the mixture is pale and thick.
3. Place the cake cases in a metal bun tray and place a heaped teaspoon of the mixture into each case. Bake for 15–18 minutes until the cakes are well risen, golden and firm to the touch.
4. Place the cakes on a cooling rack and allow to cool completely before decorating.
5. Decorate your cakes with glacé or butter icing. (You can make your own or if you are short of time buy ready-to-use icing which you can find in a variety of kinds and colours at the supermarket.)

Here are a few decorating ideas:

For a pirate party:

Top the cakes with chocolate butter icing and mark with a fork to resemble wooden decking. Make a small sail – draw on a skull and crossbones and add a party child's name – and thread the sail onto a cocktail stick. Stick a jelly baby 'Captain' into the icing on each pirate ship.

For an animal or jungle themed party:

Make the cakes into mice. Decorate half of the cupcakes with white butter icing and the remainder with chocolate butter icing. On the white iced cakes stick chocolate buttons into the icing to represent ears and on the chocolate iced cakes use white chocolate buttons. Using a tube of blue icing, add eyes. Use small jelly sweets to represent noses and short lengths of liquorice for whiskers.

'Make a wish' cakes

Decorate each cupcake with pastel icing and hundreds and thousands and place a single candle in a holder in the centre of each cake. Put a 'make a wish' cake at each place setting. Each child has to blow out the candle, close their eyes and make a secret wish. Little girls love doing this!

For a summer party

Ice the whole of the top of the cakes with blue glacé icing. Put a very small amount of demerara sugar in the centre of each cake, to represent a sandy beach, and stick a paper cocktail umbrella (you'll find them in the drinks section at supermarkets and at wine stores) in the centre of each cake.

Biscuits

Home-made biscuits are a great favourite among children. Invest in a collection of cookie cutters and you can create biscuits to suit every occasion. Either serve them plain or decorate with icing, sweets or hundreds and thousands. (Avoid gold and silver balls, they are sometimes very hard and can damage little teeth.)

Mini biscuits

(Makes about 15)

75g/3oz soft margarine
50g/2oz icing sugar
1 large egg yolk
150g/5oz plain flour
A few drops of vanilla extract

1. Preheat the oven to 180°C/Gas 4.
2. Sieve the icing sugar into a mixing bowl. Add the margarine and beat until smooth. Stir in the egg yolk and the vanilla extract. Sieve the flour into the mixture and stir until you have a smooth dough.
3. Wrap the dough in clingfilm and place in the freezer for 30 minutes. Remove from the freezer and roll out the dough on a lightly floured surface until it is 1cm/½ inch thick. Cut out biscuits using cookie cutters. Collect together the trimmings, roll out again, and make more biscuits until all of the dough is used. Place the biscuits on a nonstick baking tray and bake for 10–12 minutes or until they are lightly golden. Cool for 10 minutes on the baking tray. Lift onto a wire rack to continue cooling. When they are cold they can be iced and decorated.

Fruity crispies

These will disappear in moments!
(Makes about 36)

50g ready-to-eat apricots, finely chopped
50g sultanas
25g dried cranberries
1 tbsp golden syrup
50g/2oz butter
50g/2oz caster sugar
40g/1½ oz puffed rice cereal
A packet of paper sweet cases

1. Place the chopped apricots, cranberries and sultanas in a bowl. Add the rice cereal and mix together.
2. Melt the syrup, caster sugar and butter in a saucepan over a low heat until they are melted. Turn up the heat a little and cook for 2 minutes. Allow the mixture to cook for 5 minutes then pour over the cereal and fruit. Stir together with a wooden spoon.
3. Place heaped teaspoons of the mixture into the paper sweet cases. Allow to set for an hour.

Home-made chicken sticks and spicy potato wedges

These chicken nuggets are healthy and quick to make. Serve them with spicy potato wedges, a tomato sauce dip and a salad … perfect food for a sleepover supper. Just watch it disappear.
(Serves 6)

4 chicken breasts, skins removed
1 egg, lightly beaten
Dried fresh breadcrumbs
4 tbsp sesame seeds
2 tbsp flour
Olive oil spray
A good pinch of paprika

1. Combine the flour and paprika on one plate and the breadcrumbs and sesame seeds on another plate. Beat the egg in a shallow bowl.
2. Cut the chicken breasts into strips and coat with the flour and paprika mix. Then dip each of the strips in the egg and then into the breadcrumbs and sesame mix. Brush a nonstick baking tray with olive oil and lay the crumbed chicken strips on the tray. Lightly spray with olive spray.
3. Bake the chicken strip in the preheated oven for 15–20 minutes or until they are crisp and cooked through. Turn the strips once during the cooking time.
4. Serve with oven baked spicy potato wedges and a salad. Make the salad interesting by using little gem lettuce leaves, halved cherry tomatoes, slices of apple or pear and a sprinkling of sultanas.

CHAPTER 12
HITCH YOUR PARTY TO AN ORGANISED EVENT

A great way of partying with friends and family is to hitch your 'do' to an organised event such as a fireworks display, carnival, fête or a visit to a fair.

For example, if you are planning an afternoon visit to a fête or a sporting event why not invite your friends round for a simple brunch or buffet lunch before setting off together?

Or return home after the event for a sumptuous tea (you can get everything prepared and set out in advance) or for supper. Set out some nibbles, nuts and crisps before you leave. When you return, give your guests a glass of wine while you disappear into the kitchen to reheat a chilli con carne with rice or a casserole you made earlier.

If you are attending an evening event such as a fireworks display or an evening carnival procession, invite friends round for tea or a late afternoon barbecue before heading off for the event. Alternatively, come back after the event for a simple supper.

You'll find lots more ideas for food to serve if you want to hitch a party to an organised event in the brunches, lunches, teas, picnics and suppers sections.

Anthea's top tip

Another nice idea is to find a traditional village green cricket match and invite your guests to join you there for a simple but sophisticated picnic. It doesn't matter if you haven't mastered the rules of the game!

Bonfire party

There's nothing quite like the excitement and fun of Guy Fawkes Night to get everyone in the mood to party. Invite your guests to attend an organised fireworks display with you and then head home to continue the fun.

After a couple of hours outside on a cold November evening, everyone will be hungry, so serve food that is warm and filling. Choose dishes that can be prepared in advance and simply reheated.

Before you leave home make sure absolutely everything is ready for your return. With your guests following you in through the front door there'll be no time to plump up the cushions and clear away the clutter! And it's a good idea to see that your kitchen doesn't look as though a herd of buffalo has passed through, as guests are always anxious to lend a hand at this kind of informal event. Accept any help you can get!

⤖ Bonfire Night Menu ⤘

Spicy dips and salsa with crunchy tacos and tortilla chips
Guacamole and sour cream and chive dip

Baked jacket potatoes filled with chilli mince and grated cheese topping
Crunchy topped baked bean and sausage bake

Winter fruit compote
Greek yogurt
Or
Cream-topped hot chocolate and home-made biscuits

Drinks

Serve beers, soft drinks and hot chocolate. Don't be tempted to use canned 'squirty' cream on the top of mugs of hot chocolate – use lightly whipped fresh cream sprinkled with grated dark chocolate.

Off the shelf

To save time call in at the deli or supermarket for:
- Dips
- Salsa
- Tortilla chips
- Mulled wine
- Hand-made biscuits

Tessa's Flapjack

225g/8oz of butter
150g/5oz demerara sugar
3tbsp golden syrup
400g/14oz porridge oats
150g/5oz desiccated coconut

1. Preheat the oven to 170°C/Gas 3 and line a 20cm (8-inch) square baking tin with baking parchment.
2. Over a low heat melt the butter, demerara sugar and golden syrup together in a large saucepan.
3. Add the porridge oats and desiccated coconut and mix well together. Spoon into the prepared tin and level the top. Bake in the preheated oven until golden brown and firm to the touch.
4. Cool and cut into squares.

Crunchy topped baked bean and sausage bake
(Serves 10)

20 good-quality pork sausages
1 large onion, diced
200g/7oz button mushrooms, wiped
3 large tins baked beans
1 large tin chopped tomatoes
1–2tbsp Worcestershire sauce
Freshly ground black pepper
For the topping:
4 slices wholemeal bread, crumbed
100g/4oz mature Cheddar cheese, grated

1. Cook the sausages in the normal way, taking care not to burn them. Cut each sausage in half and set aside.
2. Place the diced onion in a large nonstick saucepan and cook for 5 to 8 minutes until lightly golden, then add the mushrooms and cook for a further 5 minutes. Add the baked beans and the chopped tomatoes to the pan. Add the Worcestershire sauce to taste, and season with freshly ground black pepper.
3. Add the sausages and bring to the boil. Simmer gently for 5 minutes.
4. Just before serving reheat the bean bake – you can do this in the microwave to save time. After it is heated sprinkle over the breadcrumbs and grated cheese and place under a hot grill until the crumbs are golden and the cheese has melted.
5. Serve with warmed crusty bread.

Anthea's top tips

Avoid the queues for the drink and refreshment stalls at firework displays – they always seem to stretch forever. Instead take along flasks of mulled wine and some crisp home-made ginger biscuits or Tessa's tasty flapjacks for your guests. Have some mulled apple juice for the children. Don't forget to take along insulated cups and cinnamon-stick stirrers.

If you must have some fireworks at home get a display box (the kind that has one fuse and gives a display lasting a few minutes). Read the instructions carefully and be sure to follow the Fireworks Code.

Remember to follow the Fireworks Code

- Keep fireworks in a sealed box or tin
- Use them one at a time, replacing the lid immediately
- NEVER put fireworks in your pocket
- Read the instructions carefully, using a torch or hand lamp – NEVER use a naked flame
- Light fireworks at arm's-length using a taper or firework lighter
- Stand well back and NEVER return to a firework after it has been lit – it could explode in your face
- Ensure that all children watching fireworks are well supervised
- NEVER throw fireworks
- Keep all pets and animals indoors
- Take care of sparklers, wear gloves to hold them and dispose of sparklers in a bucket of water as soon as they are finished – NEVER give sparklers to children under five

When buying fireworks, make sure they always comply with BS 7114 and are clearly marked for their intended use – 'Indoor, Garden or Display'.

CHAPTER 13
DOING IT FOR CHARITY

Many social events can be turned into charity fundraisers. It doesn't have to be a grand 'do' to persuade guests to be generous. Coffee mornings, lunches, teas and suppers can all be used to make money for a good cause. All you need is some simple food and some novel fundraising ideas.

Here are just a few to get you started.

Auction of promises

Ask friends and guests to offer their skills for you to auction, whether it's a hairdo, a manicure, baby-sitting, a couple of hours ironing or gardening, planning a children's party, or just an offer to wash the car. Think of some of the jobs you hate doing – the chances are others hate them as well – and persuade friends to promise these tasks for auction.

Envelope tree (or board)

Persuade friends, acquaintances and local businesses to donate prizes for example a rally-car drive, a visit to a stately home, a haircut. Then put the details of each of the prizes in separate envelopes. Put a value on the envelope (say £5, £10, £20, £50) – that is the value of the prize. Guests are invited to buy an envelope from the tree. Display the envelopes attractively on a piece of painted hardboard cut out in the shape of a tree, or a decorated notice board. Attach the envelopes with ribbon or coloured pegs.

Mystery envelope auction

Put the names of prizes that have been donated inside envelopes and then auction the mystery envelopes. This is great fun, as no one knows whether they are buying a pair of socks, or a romantic weekend for two in Paris. All they should know is the minimum and maximum possible value of the prize.

Recreate the sound of the Swinging 60s

Invite guests to wear 60s gear (or choose any other decade you fancy) and hire an entertainer for the evening. Serve a simple rustic buffet and ask guests to make donations for their suppers.

Bottle bran tub (this is one for adults only!)

Beg or borrow a large wooden packing case and decorate it. Collect together as many bottles as you can – spirits, wine, miniatures, sauce, vinegar, soft drinks and mixers – and tie pretty string round the necks of the bottles. Hang the other end of the strings over the edge of the box. Fill the box with wood shavings and invite guests to buy a string to win the bottle on the other end.

Barbecue with a cause

If you've got space at a barbecue or an 'at home' picnic set up one or two fun sideshows – stocks, 'splat the rat', coconut shy, hoopla – and let guests pay to have a go. You can often find local organisations that have sideshow equipment they use at their own events, such as the Scouts or local school, who would be willing to let you hire them.

Always be on the lookout for novel fundraising and party ideas

- Look in magazines and local newspapers to see what kind of fundraising and party ideas other people have come up with.
- If you are a member of a charity that produces a magazine, look through its news pages to see what others have done to support it.
- Search the Internet for ideas.
- Watch notice boards to see the kinds of events other people in your area are holding.

CHAPTER 14
RESOURCES

Shopping on the Internet

Shopping on the Internet can be a real time saver but remember to place your order in good time, particularly at Christmas when companies are likely to be busy and popular lines may sell out.

- Order early so that you can take advantage of standard delivery rather than express services.
- Always print out a copy of your order or confirmation of your order, in case you need to chase it up.
- Allow time to check a few websites before ordering – you could save yourself money. Or use one of the many price comparison websites to do the legwork for you.
- Only buy from websites which show a postal address and telephone number.
- Before you enter your credit card details, check that there is a padlock symbol in one of the bottom corners of the screen.
- Never reveal your PIN number over the Internet or any password associated with the card.
- If a company is new to you, you may find it among customer reviews on sites such as www.reviewcentre.co.uk and www.ciao.co.uk.

DRINKS

For orders of wines, beers and spirits
The Drink Shop
www.thedrinkshop.com

Virgin Wines
www.virgin.wines.com

Drinks Direct
www.drinksdirect.co.uk

Chateau Online (0800 169 2736)
www.chateauonline.co.uk

Majestic Wine (01923 298200)
www.majestic.co.uk

FOOD

For party food, and drinks
Waitrose (0800 188884)
www.waitrose.co.uk

Marks & Spencer (0845 302 1234)
www.marksandspencer.com

Tesco (0800 505555)
www.tesco.com

Sainsbury's (0800 636262)
www.sainsburys.co.uk

Asda (0845 300 1111)
www.asda.co.uk

Morrisons (0845 611 61111)
www.morrisons.co.uk

SPECIALIST FOODS

Quality chocolates and truffles created by some of the world top chocolatiers
www.hotelchocolat.co.uk

For haggis – traditional and vegetarian
MacSween of Edinburgh (0131 440 2555)
www.macsween.co.uk

For takeaways in your area
www.hungryhouse.co.uk

PARTY SUPPLIES

Extensive selection of party supplies for adults and children
The Party Store
www.partystore.co.uk

Tableware, balloons, character merchandise
Party Box
www.partybox.co.uk

Supplies for children's parties
Toys R Us
www.toysrus.co.uk

Themed goods for children's parties, general party supplies
Woolworths (0845 608 1102)
www.woolworths.co.uk

Party supplies, themed goods
W.H. Smith (0870 444 6444)
www.whsmith.co.uk

VENUES
Hundreds of venues to hire throughout the UK
www.perfectvenue.com

HOME SUPPLIES
The Pier (0845 609 1234)
www.pier.co.uk

The White Company (0870 900 9555)
www.thewhitecompany.com

John Lewis (0845 604 9049)
www.johnlewis.com

Habitat (0870 411 5501)
www.habitat.co.uk

Lakeland Limited (015394 88100)
www.lakelandlimited.co.uk

Debenhams (020 7408 4444)
www.debenhams.com

Homebase (0845 077 8888)
www.homebase.co.uk

Heals
www.heals.co.uk

IKEA
www.ikea.com

INFORMATION
Books for Cooks (020 7221 1992)
www.booksforcooks.com

SOME OF MY FAVOURITE COOKERY BOOKS
Jo Pratt – *In the Mood for Food* (Michael Joseph Ltd)
Nigel Slater – *Real Food* (Fourth Estate)
Jamie Oliver – *Happy Days with the Naked Chef* (Penguin)
Raymond Blanc – *Simple French Cookery* (BBC Books)
Bill Granger – *Every Day* (Murdoch Books)
Rose Gray & Ruth Rogers – *River Café Cook Book* (Ebury Press)
Rick Stein – *Seafood* (BBC Books)

IF YOU ARE A FIRST TIMER IN THE KITCHEN, THESE WILL HELP!
Rose Gray & Ruth Rogers – *River Café Cook Book Easy* (Ebury Press)
Gary Rhodes – *Step by Step Cooking* (Ebury Press)
Delia Smith – *How to Cook Book One* (BBC Books)

Index